12.95

Everyman's
Book of
Nonsense

Edited by
JOHN DAVIES

Foreword by
SPIKE MILLIGAN

J M Dent & Sons Ltd
London Melbourne Toronto

First published 1981
© Victorama Ltd. 1981

Printed in Great Britain
by Billing & Sons Ltd, Guildford, London, Oxford & Worcester
for
J.M. Dent & Sons Ltd
Aldine House, 33 Welbeck Street, London

British Library Cataloguing in Publication Data

Everyman's book of nonsense.
  1. Nonsense-verses, English
  I. Davies, John
  821'.07   PR1195.N/

ISBN 0-460-04479-6

Contents

Foreword, 15
Introduction, 17

Anonsense

As It Fell upon a Day, *21*
The Man in the Wilderness (1641), *21*
A Fancy (1656), *21*
A. Was an Archer (*c.* 1700), *22*
From Mother Goose's Melody (1756)
  Illustrated by Arthur Rackham, *22*
A Dirge, *23*
From Gammer Gurton's Garland (1784), *24*
Good King Arthur, *24*
We're All in the Dumps, *24*
The Bells of London, *24*
The Irish Pig, *26*
Death of My Aunt, *26*
Mother's Lament, *26*
Under the Drooping Willow Tree, *27*
Hexameter and Pentameter, *28*
The Sad Story of a Little Boy That Cried, *29*
Poor Beasts! *29*
Ten Thousand Years Ago, *30*
Janet Was Quite Ill One Day, *30*
I Dunno, *31*
Tale of a Stamp, *31*
I Wish I Were, *33*
Two Legs Behind and Two Before, *34*
Somewhat Alike, *34*
Life Story, *35*
The Whango Tree, *36*
What Nonsense! *37*
If You Should Meet a Crocodile, *37*

Adele Aldridge (1934–)

Three Notpoems, *38*

Woody Allen (1935–)

Mr Big, *39*
From My Philosophy, *45*

Richard Harris Barham (1788–1845)

Sir Rupert the Fearless, A Legend of Germany, *46*
    From The Ingoldsby Legends

Beachcomber (J. B. Morton) (1893–1979)

Stalemate, *55*
A Folk Song, *58*
Labour-Saving, *58*
The Case of the Twelve Red-Bearded Dwarfs, *59*

Max Beerbohm (1872–1956)

A Note on the Einstein Theory, *63*

Hilaire Belloc (1870–1953)

From The Bad Child's Book of Beasts
    and More Beasts for Worse Children:
The Marmozet, *66*
The Python, *67*

Robert Benchley (1889–1945)

Go Down, Sweet Jordan, *70*

John Betjeman (1906–)

Dorset, *73*

Niels Mogens Bodecker (1922–)

House Flies, *74*

Gyles Brandreth (1948–)

Ode to My Goldfish, *75*

Gelett Burgess (1866–1951)

'I never saw a Purple Cow', *75*

Robert Burns (1759–96)

Tam O'Shanter, *75*

Douglas Byng (1893–   )

Millie the Mermaid, *80*

George Canning (1770–1827)

Ipecacuanha, *82*

Henry Carey (1687?–1743)

Namby Pamby, *82*

Lewis Carroll (Charles Dodgson) (1832–98)

Letters, *85*
From Through the Looking-Glass – 1872:
Jabberwocky, *87*
Humpty Dumpty, *89*
Looking Glass Insects, *91*
The Walrus and the Carpenter, *92*
From Sylvie and Bruno – 1889, *97*
From Sylvie and Bruno, Concluded – 1893, *97*

G. K. Chesterton (1874–1936)

Wine and Water, *98*

Samuel Taylor Coleridge (1772–1834)

The House That Jack Built, *99*

Frank Davies (1911–   )

Song in Outer Esquimo Dialect, *99*
All Our Yesterdays, *100*

John Davies of Hereford (1565?–1618)

'If there were, oh! an Hellespont of cream', *100*

8

Charles Dickens (1812–70)

From Pickwick Papers, *101*
From Nicholas Nickleby, *106*

W. C. Fields (1879–1946)

From Never Give a Sucker an Even Break, *107*

Samuel Foote (1720–77)

The Grand Panjamdrum, *111*

W. S. Gilbert (1836–1911)

The Student, *111*
   From The Bab Ballads

A. D. Godley (1856–1925)

On the Motor Bus, *114*
In Memoriam Examinatoris Cuiusdam, *114*

Oliver Goldsmith (1728–74)

Elegy on the Death of a Mad Dog, *115*

Harry Graham (1874–1936)

   Illustrated by 'G. H.' and Ridgewell
The Stern Parent, *117*
L'Enfant Glacé, *118*

Robert Graves (1895–   )

A Grotesque, *118*

W. Heath Robinson (1896–1944)

The New Diving Boat, *119*
High Tide, *120*

A. P. Herbert (1890–1971)

Plum's Dying Speech, *120*
   From Two Gentlemen of Soho

Dr Heinrich Hoffman (1809–94)

The Story of Augustus, *121*

Gerard Hoffnung (1925–59)

The Organ, *124*
The Horn, *125*
The Tenor, *125*
A Hum, *126*

Oliver Wendell Holmes (1809–94)

The Last Laugh, *126*

A. E. Housman (1859–1936)

 Illustrated by Tomi Ungerer
On the Death of a Female Officer of the Salvation Army, *127*

Ted Hughes (1930–   )

My Uncle Dan, *128*

Christopher Isherwood (1904–   )

The Common Cormorant, *128*

ITMA by Ted Kavanagh (1894–1958), *129*

Paul Jennings (1918–   )

Galoshes, *134*

Samuel Johnson (1709–84)

Hermit Hoar, *135*

John Keats (1795–1821)

From A Song of Myself, *135*

Stephen Leacock (1869–1944)

The Awful Fate of Melpomenus Jones, *137*

Edward Lear (1812–88)

The Owl and the Pussy-cat, *139*
The Duck and the Kangaroo, *140*
From The Story of the Four Little Children
    Who Went Round the World, *142*
The Jumblies, *144*
Nonsense Botany, *147*

John Lennon (1940–   )

I Sat Belonely down a Tree, *151*

Dan Leno (George Galvin) (1860–1904)

From The Hampton Court Maze, *151*
From Our Stoves, *152*

C. S. Lewis (1898–1963)

Awake, My Lute! *153*

Vachel Lindsay (1879–1931)

The Daniel Jazz, *154*

Hugh Lofting (1886–1947)

From Gub Gub's Book, *156*

Archibald MacLeish (1892–   )

Mother Goose's Garland, *157*

Walter de la Mare (1873–1956)

Green, *158*
The Bards, *158*

Don Marquis (1878–1937)

the coming of archy, *158*
aesop revised by archy, *160*

Roger McGough (1937–   )

From Sporting Relations, *163*

Spike Milligan (1918–)

Main Characters from The Goon Show, *164*
The Telephone (*with Larry Stephens*), *165*
The Skate, *167*

Adrian Mitchell (1932–)

The Apeman's Hairy Body Song, *167*

Monty Python

From The Brand New Monty Python Bok — 1973:
Rat Recipes, *167*
From Norman Henderson's Diary, *168*

Edwin Morgan (1920–)

The Computer's First Christmas Card, *169*

Ogden Nash (1902–71)

The Poultries, *170*
Thoughts Thought, *171*
The Private Dining-room, *172*
The Pig, *173*
The Kangaroo, *173*

Flann O'Brien (1911–66)

From The Best of Myles na Gopaleen:
The Dublin Waama League's Escort Service, *173*
The Myles na Gopaleen Catechism of Cliché, *174*

Ann O'Connor (?–)

Rhubarb Ted, *175*

Philip O'Connor (1916–)

Poems, *175*

Brian Patten (1946–)

Little Johnny's Confession, *178*

Mervyn Peake (1911–68)

O Love! O Death! O Ecastasy! *179*
O Here It Is and There It Is, *180*
I Have My Price, *181*
I Waxes and I Wanes, Sir, *181*

John Phoenix (George H. Derby) (1824–61)

Phoenix's Pictorial, *182*

Sylvia Plath (1932–63)

Metaphors, *185*

Roger Price (1921–)

Droodles, *186*

Alexander Resnikoff (1894–)

Two Witches, *187*

Moss Rich (1920–)

Instructions for Using Your Japanese Pocket Calculator, *187*

Robert Robinson (1927–)

Doggerel, *188*

Christina Rossetti (1830–94)

Fishy Tale, *189*

W. C. Sellar (?–1951) and R. J. Yeatman (?–1968)

Illustrated by John Leech and John Reynolds
From 1066 And All That, *189*

Robert Service (1874–1958)

The Bread-Knife Ballad, *192*

William Shakespeare (1564–1616)

From Love's Labour's Lost, *193*
From The Winter's Tale, *196*

Timothy Shy (D. B. Wyndham Lewis) (1894–1969)

Variations on a Simple Theme, *196*

Peter Simple (Michael Wharton) (1913–)

'Pop Notes' by Jim Droolberg, *200*
Realism, *201*

N. F. Simpson (1919–)

From At Least It's a Precaution against Fire, *202*

John Skelton (1460–1529)

Mannerly Margery Milk and Ale, *204*
To Mistress Margaret Hussey, *205*

Stevie Smith (1903–71)

Tenuous and Precarious, *206*
The Grange, *207*

Jonathan Swift (1667–1745)

Verses Made for Women Who Cry Apples, &c, *208*

William Makepeace Thackeray (1811–63)

A Tragic Story, *210*

Dylan Thomas (1914–53)

From Holiday Memory, *211*

J. R. R. Tolkein (1892–1973)

The Man in the Moon Stayed up Too Late, *212*

Mark Twain (Samuel Clemens) (1835–1910)

Our Italian Guide, *214*

14

Stanley Unwin (1911–)

On the Subject of TV and Radio Reception,
and Hearing the News in Dutch, *218*

John Updike (1932–)

Superman, *218*

J. J. Webster (1920–)

La Forza del Destino (The Force of Destiny), *219*

Reed Whittemore (1919–)

The Party, *219*

T. H. White (1906–64)

The Witch's Work Song, *220*

Robb Wilton (1881–1957)

From Back Answers, *221*

Biographical Notes, 222
Index of Titles and First Lines, 237
Acknowledgments, 249

Foreword

Nonsense. The word allows the mind, the soul, the written word, the painting – all art forms – access to anything. At first one would believe that nonsense would have to be artificially created, i.e. one never sees a work of nature that calls for the description 'nonsense'. Yet man can apply himself to nature and create a situation that is nonsense. For instance, in Australia literally all the wood chip industry is exported to Japan (the Japanese having chopped all their own trees down), in turn, Japan pulps the wood into paper which is made into glossy brochures extolling the delights of the Suzuki motor bike, solid state transistors (more nonsense), which are sent back to Australia, who in turn buys the products advertised therein. Nonsense?

The computer! This would appear to be the solution to our back logs, in a flash it will tell you your overdraft, your National Health Card No., etc. etc. – brilliant – also in a flash the computer sent an old age pensioner in Finchley a quarterly gas bill for £48,000. Nonsense? Whereas, at one time nonsense had not filtered into our world of commerce and bureaucracy, it was a delight to release our inner tensions by uttering or performing nonsense, children do it all the time. Likewise reading it. An early nonsense writer was Thomas Hood whose lines about a soldier:

> Who in war's alarums,
> A Cannonball took off his legs
> So he laid down his arms.

made me fall into helpless laughter at school — what joy to come upon the undoing of logic, and from it bring forth mirth. Of course there are adjuncts of Nonsense. Surrealism has an element of nonsense. Art – a large measure of 'modern' art is sheer nonsense. At an exhibition of modern Japanese art in Nagoya I saw a boot, on a plane, with a carrot growing out of it entitled 'Spring'. Absolute nonsense. The fact that the artist didn't think so, made it even greater nonsense. *He* was nonsense as well.

Lear — a childhood hero — sublimated his superb draughtsmanship to add ill-drawn caricatures to his limericks. When Picasso did it after his 'blue' period — it was great modern art. I took my children to see some of Henry Moore's chunky abstract sculptures in Hyde Park. My daughter Laura, 7, said, 'Look something's fallen off a Jumbo Jet'. Out of the mouths of babes . . .

The extraordinary part of nonsense is that only a small percentage of people gain pleasure from it. I think this is the result of a humour-less upbringing. I notice that nonsense is always acceptable to the young—clowning is part of nonsense. I have tried it successfully with children of *all* races and 99 per cent have always laughed, and even tried to imitate me. But then I have sat with men, intellectuals, who are totally baffled by nonsense. I was once with an American reporter from *Time Life* at dinner. I had ordered Venison. When I was eating it he said: 'Is that Deer?'. I said: 'Very, it's nearly £7 a portion'. His reaction was (and dead serious), 'No, you misunderstand me, I meant D-E-E-R, not D-E-A-R, etc.' The man left an indelible blank on my mind.

Throughout the history of man there have been dim adumbrations of attempts at nonsense, using animals posturing as humans — often seen in the later Egyptian dynasty tomb paintings, likewise in Pompeii. Greek drama used it: their idea of nonsense — a clown with a giant hanging phallus with brightly coloured spots which were constantly being kicked. People to this day say 'we knocked spots off him', not knowing they are referring to those past clowns — culinary experts to this day don't know that 'Spotted Dick' has its antecedence in those Greek plays.

The nonsense school has been the last of the creative arts to surface — who would have understood the Marx Brothers in 1830 — or even 1880? It is among the most difficult of the arts to be accepted at a classical level. Hence there is no Chair of Humour in any University (which in itself is absurd) — however, it seems to have survived and developed without academic aid. And so to the book — in it there's a plethora of writers and artists. Plough through it. If you enjoy it — pride yourself on having a sense of nonsense. If you don't — choose a convenient cliff and jump off — I promise the rocks will break your fall.

Spike Milligan

Introduction

Once upon a time, this book was longer than it is now. Cutting it to a reasonable length made us ask: should we cut the things that aren't quite so funny as others, or the things that show traces of sense? If a piece is intended to be nonsense but isn't amusing should it go in? Should things go in when they are very funny but on the borderline between nonsense and fantasy? In short, what *is* nonsense? For the purposes of producing an anthology of manageable proportions, we (a happy team of researchers, and myself) came up with a simple definition of our kind of nonsense: it is 'something that makes no sense, but raises a smile.'

Soon after formulating this definition we realized that it embraced a large part of all the prose, verse and art in the world. With great regret we have had to exclude most of all three. To put our task into the realm of the possible we decided to start our work by *excluding* four types of 'nonsense'.

The first is unintentional nonsense. There are so many good examples of nonsense masquerading as sound sense – be it in the shape of incomprehensible documentation issued by the Department of Health and Social Security or outlandishly obscurantist academic criticism (there really *is* a book called *The Meaning of Meaning*) — that the genre deserves an anthology of its own. Having decided to exclude unintentional nonsense, we had no alternative but to leave out the likes of William McGonagall, the mighty Scots bard, much of whose work makes little sense and raises a very broad smile. However since that certainly was not his intention, we could not honestly find room for him here. (That said, we still want to devote half an inch to him and two of the most engagingly ambiguous lines in literature:

> Immortal! William Shakespeare, there's none can you excel,
> You have drawn out your characters remarkably well. . .)

The second literary form we decided to avoid was the limerick. We came across hundreds that could be classified as nonsense, but since we couldn't include them all, we decided we wouldn't include any.

We decided to exclude 'nursery nonsense' as well, unless it happened to be 'nursery nonsense' that came downstairs with us as we grew up — which is why the Owl and the Pussycat are here, but the Cat and the Fiddle aren't.

We decided too that translations were taboo. For no very good reason, apart from the fact that the translation is even more nonsensical than the original, we have made one exception to this rule. Frank Davies, the great authority on Greenland, and a scholar of its languages, has supplied us specially with a translation of a short piece written in the Esquimo dialect, Rebbulberomton.

Having decided what to leave out, we were still left with several million words of nonsense from which to make our selection. Determined to make this the 'ultimate' in nonsense anthologies we have naturally chosen the *best* nonsense we could find, and by 'best' we mean, of course, the nonsense that appealed to us most. In the pages that follow you will find contributions from all the acknowledged masters of nonsense from both sides of the Atlantic, but alongside the familiar names of Edward Lear and Lewis Carroll and W. S. Gilbert, of Mark Twain and Ogden Nash and Stephen Leacock, you will find pieces by writers whose names are certainly familiar but whose work is not usually nonsensical. You do not automatically think of Shakespeare or Keats, or even of Dickens or Thackeray, as nonsense writers, but there can be no doubt that they have a place here.

Many of the most respected anthologies of this kind give understandable (but perhaps undue) weight to the more revered writers of the genre and leave the impression that the nineteenth century was the undoubted golden age of nonsense. Well, certainly the Georgians had Richard Harris Barham and Samuel Taylor Coleridge and the Victorians had the twin colossi of Lear and Carroll, and all are represented here, but can any century match the twentieth's nonsense line-up? Woody Allen, Max Beerbohm, Hilaire Belloc, Robert Benchley, Gelett Burgess, Harry Graham, A. P. Herbert, John Lennon, Don Marquis, J. B. Morton, Mervyn Peake, N. F. Simpson — not to mention Spike Milligan (since he will be mentioning himself in his Foreword) – are true masters of the form, each of whose work as seen here makes very little sense and raises smiles quite as broad as — no let's be honest, a lot broader than — those generated by the work of their predecessors.

Alongside the nonsense from twentieth-century poets and novelists better known for their more serious work (Betjeman, Chesterton, Graves, Housman, Ted Hughes, Christopher Isherwood, C. S. Lewis, Walter de la Mare, Archibald MacLeish, Roger McGough, Adrian Mitchell, Edwin Morgan, Brian Patten, Sylvia Plath, Stevie Smith, old Uncle John Updike and all) we have taken particular pleasure in including a selection of the nonsense of *performers* rather than writers, running from the great turn-of-the-century music hall and pantomime star Dan Leno through to the contemporary prince of pseudo-semantic byplay, Professor Stanley Unwin, via ITMA and Monty Python, Robb Wilton and W. C. Fields.

While most readers will agree that everything included in this anthology can fairly be described as nonsense, not everyone will approve of our selection. We could have filled the whole book with Edward Lear and Lewis Carroll, but we were determined to make room for the less familiar even at the expense of old favourites from the pens of the 'classic nonsense' writers. For examples, there wasn't space for 'You are old, Father William' *and* Douglas Byng's 'Millie the Mermaid', so we decided to include the latter (specially revised by Mr Byng for this collection), thinking it might give you a pleasant surprise, and drop the former, guessing you would know it by heart anyway.

Anthologists with only a set number of pages at their disposal have to be ruthless and fearless and prepared to make mistakes. Why no T. S. Eliot? Why no Joyce? Why no Marx? Well, in the end we decided that Eliot's light verse was humorous rather than nonsensical and that 'The Ballad of Perse O'Reilly' from *Finnegan's Wake* (our Joyce candidate) didn't raise much of a smile. (Several verses by Swinburne and Thomas Hood were also on the short-list, but also ultimately failed the smile-test). As to Marx, I have to report that when *The Groucho Letters* got lost in the post we consulted Mr Marx through a spirit medium to see what we should do. He told us he wouldn't want to be in *any* book to which he was a contributor. (We have to say here, 'And Karl Marx didn't reply at all'.) To solve the problem of including the Marx Brothers without including them we have found space for Harpo's speech from 'A Night At The Opera', which you will find on page 400.

What we do have that other collections of nonsense tend to exclude are illustrations. 'What is the use of a book' said Alice, 'without pictures or conversations?' She was quite right, of course, and that is why you will find the pages that follow packed both with nonsensical conversations and with the delicious visual nonsense of Adele Aldridge, W. Heath Robinson, Gerard Hoffnung, Mervyn Peake and many others.

Explaining the attraction of nonsense — visual or verbal — isn't easy. A fellow nonsense anthologist, Geoffrey Grigson, may have put his finger on it when he said: 'Nonsense can impart feeling.' When it does, it imparts feeling without the irrelevancies of moral comment and social awareness, without preaching or moaning. The fact that nonsense can and does impart feeling is part of what makes it so beguiling — and so frustrating. It seems to be saying something without saying anything. Perhaps the author of *The Meaning of Meaning* would be able to explain. This trickery, pretending to enlighten us when it is 'merely' entertaining us, is put to good use by the masters of the art, and you will find plenty of them hard at work in the pages that follow — and if they manage 'merely' to entertain you, then we will consider ours a job well done.

In true nonsense fashion we have saved discussing our first decision till last: the matter of beginning at the beginning. As we decided not to include translations, the only problem was where to begin with English nonsense. To a modern reader, would Chaucer without a translation seem like unintentional nonsense? Rather than risk contravening our rules at the outset, it seemed wiser to move forward a little and begin with John Skelton, Poet Laureate to both Universities, tutor to Henry VIII, and a prince of nonsense. Skelton is our earliest contributor, but since the material is presented alphabetically, the varied works of that equally gifted versifier Anon come first. Who was he? Who was *she*? We don't know, but if you can help us identify (and date) the author of any of the pieces presented anonymously here, we would be most grateful. Anon has, of course, been writing for longer — and in many instances, better! — than any of the other contributors to this anthology, but that is no reason for us not to nail him if we can.

John Davies

Anonsense

As It Fell upon a Day

As I was sitting on the hearth
(*And O, but a hog is fat!*)
A man came hurrying up the path,
(*And what care I for that?*)

When he came the house unto,
His breath both quick and short he drew.

When he came before the door,
His face grew paler than before.

When he turned the handle round,
The man fell fainting to the ground.

When he crossed the lofty hall,
Once and again I heard him fall.

When he came up to the turret stair,
He shrieked and tore his raven hair.

When he came my chamber in,
(*And O, but a hog is fat!*)
I ran him through with a golden pin,
(*And what care I for that?*)

The Man in the Wilderness (1641)

The man in the wilderness asked of me,
How many strawberries grow in the sea?
I answered him as I thought good,
As many red herrings as grow in the wood.

A Fancy (1656)

When Piecrust first began to reign,
  Cheese-parings went to war,
Red Herrings lookt both blue and wan,
  Green Leeks and Puddings jar.

Blind Hugh went out to see
  Two cripples run a race,
The Ox fought with the Humble Bee
  And claw'd him by the face.

A. Was an Archer (*c.* 1700)

A was an Archer, and shot at a frog,
B was a Blindman, and led by a dog.
C was a Cutpurse, and lived in disgrace,
D was a Drunkard, and had a red face.
E was an eater, a glutton was he,
F was a Fighter, and fought with a flea.
G was a Giant, and pulled down a house,
H was a Hunter, and hunted a mouse.
I was an Ill man, and hated by all
K was a Knave, and he robbed great and small.
L was a Liar, and told many lies,
M was a Madman, and beat out his eyes.
N was a Nobleman, nobly born,
O was an Ostler, and stole horses' corn.
P was a Pedlar, and sold many pins,
Q was a Quarreller, and broke both his shins.
R was a Rogue, and ran about town,
S was a Sailor, a man of renown.
T was a Tailor, and knavishly bent,
U was a Usurer, took ten per cent.
W was a Writer, and money he earned,
X was one Xenophon, prudent and learned.
Y was a Yeoman, and worked for his bread,
Z was one Zeno the Great, but he's dead.

From Mother Goose's Melody (1765)

Illustrated by Arthur Rackham

Three wise men of Gotham
Went to sea in a bowl:
And if the bowl had been stronger,
My song would have been longer.

A Dirge (1765)

Little Betty Winkle she had a pig,
It was a little pig not very big;
When he was alive he liv'd in clover,
But now he's dead and that's all over;
Johnny Winkle he
Sat down and cry'd,
Betty Winkle she
Laid down and dy'd;
So there was an end of one, two and three,
Johnny Winkle he,
Betty Winkle she,
And Piggy Wiggie.

From Gammer Gurton's Garland (1784)

Come, let's to bed, says Sleepy-head;
Tarry a while, says Slow;
Put on the pot, says Greedy-gut,
We'll sup before we go.

Good King Arthur

When good King Arthur ruled this land,
    He was a goodly king;
He stole three pecks of barley-meal,
    To make a bag-pudding.

A bag-pudding the king did make,
    And stuff'd it well with plums;
And in it put great lumps of fat,
    As big as my two thumbs.

The king and queen did eat thereof,
    And noblemen beside;
And what they could not eat that night,
    The queen next morning fried.

We're All in the Dumps

We're all in the dumps,
For diamonds are trumps,
The kittens are gone to St Paul's,
The babies are bit,
The moon's in a fit,
And the houses are built without walls.

The Bells of London

Gay go up and gay go down,
To ring the bells of London Town.

Bull's eyes and targets,
Say the bells of St Margaret's.

Brickbats and tiles,
Say the bells of St Giles'.

Halfpence and farthings,
Say the bells of St Martin's.

Oranges and lemons,
Say the bells of St Clement's.

Pancakes and fritters,
Say the bells of St Peter's.

Two sticks and an apple,
Say the bells at Whitechapel.

Old Father Baldpate,
Say the slow bells at Aldgate.

Pokers and tongs,
Say the bells of St John's.

Kettles and pans,
Say the bells of St Anne's.

You owe me ten shillings,
Say the bells of St Helen's.

When will you pay me?
Say the bells at Old Bailey.

When I grow rich,
Say the bells at Shoreditch.

Pray when will that be?
Say the bells of Stepney.

I am sure I don't know,
Says the great bell at Bow.

Here comes the candle to light
    you to bed,
And here comes the chopper
    to chop off your head.

The Irish Pig

'Twas an evening in November,
As I very well remember,
I was strolling down the street in drunken pride,
But my knees were all a'flutter
So I landed in the gutter,
And a pig came up and lay down by my side.

Yes I lay there in the gutter
Thinking thoughts I could not utter,
When a colleen passing by did softly say,
'Ye can tell a man that boozes
By the company he chooses' —
At that, the pig got up and walked away!

Death of My Aunt

My aunt she died a month ago,
    And left me all her riches,
A feather-bed and a wooden leg,
    And a pair of calico breeches;
A coffee-pot without a spout,
    A mug without a handle,
A baccy box without a lid,
    And half a farthing candle.

Mother's Lament

A muvver was barfin' 'er biby one night,
The youngest of ten and a delicut mite,
The muvver was pore an' the biby was thin,
'Twas naught but an skelington covered in skin;
The muvver turned rahnd for the soap orf the rack,
She was only a moment, but when she turned back,
The biby was gorn; and in anguish she cried —
'OH! WHERE 'AS MY BIBY GORN?' — And the angels
        replied . . .

'Oh your biby 'as gorn dawn the plug-'ole,
  Your biby 'as gorn dawn the plug;
The poor littul fing was so skinny an' thin
'E should 'a been washed in a jug.
Your biby is perfectly 'appy,
  'E won't need a barf any more,
'E's a-muckin' abaht wiv the angels above,
  Not lorst, but gorn before.'

Under the Drooping Willow Tree

On a small six-acre farm dwelt John Grist the miller,
Near a pond not far beyond grew a drooping willow,
Underneath its spreading leaves sat Jane, his only daughter,
Meditating suicide in the muddy water.
Element Aqua Pura, Aqua Impura.
She sat by a duck pond of dark water,
Under the drooping willow tree.

She'd been jilted by a youth who had joined the Rifles,
A young man not worth a rap, who never stuck at trifles.
Though he promised to keep true, act like a faithful lover,
When his rifle suit he got, then leg bail he gave her,
Hooked it, stepped it, toddled, mizzled.
She sat by a duck pond of dark water,
Under the drooping willow tree.

'All alone I'm left,' says she, 'my poor heart is bursting;
Dearly did I love my Joe, though he wore plain fustian.
But my nose is out of joint, and don't it make me nettled.
In this pond I'll drown myself, then I shall be settled,
Bottled, finished, done for, flummoxed.'
She sat by a duck pond of dark water,
Under the drooping willow tree.

She'd no wish to spoil her clothes, so undressed that minute;
But the water felt so cold when her toes were in it.
'If it weren't so cold,' said she, 'I'd jump in like winking.'
Then she wiped her nose, and sat upon the edge thinking,
Pondering, puzzling, considering, ruminating.

She sat by a duck pond of dark water,
Under the drooping willow tree.

Like Venus she sat in her nude state staying;
Presently she was frightened by a donkey braying.
Like a frog she gave a leap, but worse luck she stumbled,
Lost her equilibrium, and in the water tumbled,
Fell in, pitched in, dropped in, popped in.
She fell in the duck pond of dark water,
Under the drooping willow tree.

When she found she'd fallen in, she then took to swooning;
Very long it would not have been, before she took to drowning.
But her Joseph was close by, saw her in the water,
With his crooked walking stick by the wool he caught her,
Nabbed her, grabbed her, seized her, collared her
From out of the duck pond of dark water,
Under the drooping willow tree.

He beheld her coming to with great acclamation,
And the tree bore witness to their reconciliation.
There it stands in all its pride, and will stand, moreover,
Unless the spot should be required by the London, Chatham
    and Dover
Railway Company, Limited, Good Dividends.
They'll sit by the duck pond of dark water,
Under the drooping willow tree.

Hexameter and Pentameter

Down in a deep dark ditch sat an old cow
    munching a beanstalk.
Out of her mouth came forth strawberry,
    strawberry froth.

The Sad Story of a Little Boy That Cried

Once a little boy, Jack, was, oh! ever so good,
Till he took a strange notion to cry all he could.

So he cried all the day, and he cried all the night,
He cried in the morning, and in the twilight;

He cried till his voice was as hoarse as a crow,
And his mouth grew so large it looked like a great O.

It grew at the bottom, and grew at the top;
It grew till they thought that it never would stop.

Each day his great mouth grew taller and taller,
And his dear little self grew smaller and smaller.

At last, that same mouth grew so big that — alack! —
It was only a mouth with a border of Jack.

Poor Beasts!

The horse and the mule live thirty years
And nothing know of wines and beers.
The goat and sheep at twenty die
And never taste of Scotch or Rye.
The cow drinks water by the ton
And at eighteen is mostly done.
The dog at fifteen cashes in
Without the aid of rum and gin.
The cat in milk and water soaks
And then in twelve short years it croaks.
The modest, sober, bone-dry hen
Lays eggs for nogs, then dies at ten.
All animals are strictly dry:
They sinless live and swiftly die;
But sinful, ginful, rum-soaked men
Survive for three score years and ten.
And some of them, a very few,
Stay pickled till they're ninety-two.

Ten Thousand Years Ago
American Nonsense Song

I was born about ten thousand years ago,
And there's nothing in this world I do not know;
 I saw Balaam on his mule
 Ridin' off to Sunday school,
And I'll lick the guy who says it isn't so.

I taught Solomon his little A-B-Cs,
I was there when they first made Limburger cheese;
 I was sailing down the bay,
 With Methuselah one day,
And I saw his whiskers waving in the breeze.

Queen Elizabeth she fell in love with me,
We were married in Milwaukee secretly;
 I was in an airplane flying
 When George Washington stopped lying,
And I once held Cleopatra on my knee.

I was there when Satan looked the garden o'er,
I saw Eve and Adam driven from the door;
 I was behind the bushes peekin'
 At the apple they was eatin'
And I swear that I'm the guy who ate the core.

Janet Was Quite Ill One Day

JANet was quite ill one day.
FEBrile troubles came her way.
MARtyr-like, she lay in bed;
APRoned nurses softly sped.
MAYbe, said the leech judicial,
JUNket would be beneficial.
JULeps, too, though freely tried,
AUGured ill, for Janet died.
SEPulchre was sadly made;
OCTaves pealed and prayers were said.
NOVices with many a tear
DECorated Janet's bier.

I Dunno

I sometimes think I'd rather crow
And be a rooster than to roost
And be a crow. But I dunno.

A rooster he can roost also,
Which don't seem fair when crows can't crow.
Which may help some. Still I dunno.

Crows should be glad of one thing though;
Nobody thinks of eating crow,
While roosters they are good enough
For anyone unless they're tough.

There's lots of tough old roosters though.
And anyway a crow can't crow,
So mebby roosters stand more show.
It looks that way. But I dunno.

Tale of a Stamp

I'm a stamp —
A postage stamp —
A two-center;
Don't want to brag,
But I never was
Licked
Except once;
By a gentleman, too;
He put me on
To a good thing;
It was an envelope —
Perfumed, pink, square.
I've been stuck on
That envelope
Ever since;
He dropped us —
The envelope and me —
Through a slot in a dark box;
But we were rescued

By a mail clerk;
More's the pity.
He hit me an awful
Smash with a hammer;
It left my face
Black and blue;
Then I went on a long
Journey
Of two days!
And when we arrived —
The pink envelope and me —
We were presented
To a perfect love
Of a girl,
With the stunningest pair
Of blue eyes
That ever blinked;
Say, she's a dream!
Well, she mutilated
The pink envelope
And tore one corner
Of me off
With a hairpin;
Then she read what
Was inside
The pink envelope.
I never saw a girl blush
So beautifully!
I would be stuck
On her – if I could.
Well, she placed
The writing back
In the pink envelope;
Then she kissed me.
O, you little godlets!
Her lips were ripe
As cherries.
And warm
As the summer sun.
We —
The pink envelope and me —
Are now

Nestling snugly
In her bosom;
We can hear
Her heart throb;
When it goes fastest
She takes us out
And kisses me.
Oh, say
This is great!
I'm glad
I'm a stamp —

A two-center.

I Wish I Were

I wish I were a
Elephantiaphus
And could pick off the coconuts with my nose
But, oh! I am not,
(Alas! I cannot be)
An Elephanti-
Elephantiaphus.
But I'm a cockroach
And I'm a water-bug,
I can crawl around and hide behind the sink.

I wish I were a
Rhinoscereeacus
And could wear an ivory toothpick in my nose
But, oh! I am not,
(Alas! I cannot be)
A Rhinoscori-
Rhinoscereeacus.
But I'm a beetle
And I'm a pumpkin-bug,
I can buzz and bang my head against the wall.

I wish I were a
Hippopopotamus
And could swim the Tigris and the broad Ganges.

But, oh! I am not,
(Alas! I cannot be)
A hippopopo-
Hippopopopotamus.
But I'm a grasshopper
And I'm a katydid,
I can play the fiddle with my left hind-leg.

I wish I were a
Levileviathan
And had seven hundred knuckles in my spine.
But, oh! I am not,
(Alas! I cannot be)
A levi-ikey-
A levi-ikey-mo
But I'm a lightning-bug,
I can light cheroots and gaspers with my tail.

Two Legs Behind and Two Before

On mules we find two legs behind,
    And two we find before;
We stand behind before we find
    What the two behind be for.
When we're behind the two behind,
    We find what these be for;
So stand before the two behind,
    And behind the two before.

Somewhat Alike

The gum-chewing student,
The cud-chewing cow,
Are somewhat alike,
Yet different somehow.
Just what is the difference —
I think I know now —
It's the thoughtful look
On the face of the cow.

Life Story

Once — but no matter when —
   There lived — no matter where —
A man, whose name — but then
   I need not that declare.

He — well, he had been born,
   And so he was alive;
His age — I details scorn —
   Was somethingty and five.

He lived — how many years
   I truly can't decide;
But this one fact appears
   He lived — until he died.

'He died,' I have averred,
   But cannot prove 'twas so,
But that he was interred,
   At any rate, I know.

I fancy he'd a son,
   I hear he had a wife:
Perhaps he'd more than one,
   I know not, on my life!

But whether he was rich,
   Or whether he was poor,
Or neither — both — or which,
   I cannot say, I'm sure.

I can't recall his name,
   Or what he used to do:
But then — well, such is fame!
   'Twill so serve me and you.

And that is why I thus,
   About this unknown man
Would fain create a fuss,
   To rescue, if I can.

From dark oblivion's blow,
   Some record of his lot:
But, ah! I do not know
   Who — where — when — why — or what.

The Whango Tree

The woggly bird sat on the whango tree,
   Nooping the rinkum corn,
And graper and graper, alas! grew he,
   And cursed the day he was born.
His crute was clum and his voice was rum,
   As curiously thur sang he,
'Oh, would I'd been rammed and eternally
     clammed
Ere I perched on this whango tree.'

Now the whango tree had a bubbly thorn,
   As sharp as a nootie's bill,
And it stuck in the woggly bird's umptum lorn
   And weepadge, the smart did thrill.
He fumbled and cursed, but that wasn't the worst,
   For he couldn't at all get free,
And he cried, 'I am gammed, and injustibly
     nammed
On the luggardly whango tree.'

And there he sits still, with no worm in his bill,
   Nor no guggledom in his nest;
He is hungry and bare, and gobliddered with care,
   And his grabbles gives him no rest;
He is weary and sore and his tugmut is raw
   And nothing to nob has he,
As he chirps, 'I am blammed and corruptibly jammed,
In this cuggerdom whango tree.'

What Nonsense!

One fine October morning
    In September, last July,
The moon lay thick upon the ground,
    The snow shone in the sky;
The flowers were singing gaily
    And the birds were in full bloom,
I went down to the cellar
    To sweep the upstairs room.

If You Should Meet a Crocodile

If you should meet a crocodile,
    Don't take a stick and poke him;
Ignore the welcome in his smile,
    Be careful not to stroke him.
For as he sleeps upon the Nile,
    He thinner gets and thinner;
And whene'er you meet a crocodile
    He's ready for his dinner.

Adele Aldridge (1934–   )

Three Notpoems

EAT
EAT
EAT
EAT
EAT
FAT
FAT
FAT
FAT_{AL}

DOGS
DO
DO
DO

TEACH
TEACH
TAEHC
CHEAT
CHEAT
CHEAT
CHEAT

Woody Allen (1935–   )

Mr Big

I was sitting in my office, cleaning the debris out of my thirty-eight
and wondering where my next case was coming from. I like being a
private eye, and even though once in a while I've had my gums
massaged with an automobile jack, the sweet smell of greenbacks
makes it all worth it. Not to mention the dames, which are a minor
preoccupation of mine that I rank just ahead of breathing. That's why,
when the door to my office swung open and a long-haired blonde
named Heather Butkiss came striding in and told me she was a nudie
model and needed my help, my salivary glands shifted into third. She
wore a short skirt and a tight sweater and her figure described a set of
parabolas that could cause cardiac arrest in a yak.

'What can I do for you, sugar?'

'I want you to find someone for me.'

'Missing person? Have you tried the police?'

'Not exactly, Mr Lupowitz.'

'Call me Kaiser, sugar. All right, so what's the scam?'

'God.'

'God?'

'That's right, God. The Creator, the Underlying Principle, the First
Cause of Things, the All Encompassing. I want you to find Him for
me.'

I've had some fruit cakes up in the office before, but when they're
built like she was, you listened.

'Why?'

'That's my business, Kaiser. You just find Him.'

'I'm sorry, sugar. You got the wrong boy.'

'But why?'

'Unless I know all the facts,' I said, rising.

'O.K., O.K.,' she said, biting her lower lip. She straightened the
seam of her stocking, which was strictly for my benefit, but I wasn't
buying any at the moment.

'Let's have it on the line, sugar.'

'Well, the truth is — I'm not really a nudie model.'

'No?'

'No. My name is not Heather Butkiss, either. It's Claire Rosensweig
and I'm a student at Vassar. Philosophy major. History of Western
Thought and all that. I have a paper due January. On Western religion.

All the other kids in the course will hand in speculative papers. But I want to *know*. Professor Grebanier said if anyone finds out for sure, they're a cinch to pass the course. And my dad's promised me a Mercedes if I get straight A's.'

I opened a deck of Luckies and a pack of gum and had one of each. Her story was beginning to interest me. Spoiled coed. High IQ and a body I wanted to know better.

'What does God look like?'

'I've never seen him,'

'Well, how do you know He exists?'

'That's for you to find out.'

'Oh, great. Then you don't know what he looks like? Or where to begin looking?'

'No. Not really. Although I suspect he's everywhere. In the air, in every flower, in you and I — and in this chair.'

'Uh huh.' So she was a pantheist. I made a mental note of it and said I'd give her case a try — for a hundred bucks a day, expenses, and a dinner date. She smiled and okayed the deal. We rode down in the elevator together. Outside it was getting dark. Maybe God did exist and maybe He didn't, but somewhere in that city there were sure a lot of guys who were going to try and keep me from finding out.

My first lead was Rabbi Itzhak Wiseman, a local cleric who owed me a favour for finding out who was rubbing pork on his hat. I knew something was wrong when I spoke to him because he was scared. Real scared.

'Of course there's a you-know-what, but I'm not even allowed to say His name or He'll strike me dead, which I could never understand why someone is so touchy about having his name said.'

'You ever see Him?'

'Me? Are you kidding? I'm lucky if I get to see my grandchildren.'

'Then how do you know He exists?'

'How do I know? What kind of question is that? Could I get a suit like this for fourteen dollars if there was no one up there? Here, feel a gabardine — how can you doubt?'

'You got nothing more to go on?'

'Hey — what's the Old Testament? Chopped liver? How do you think Moses got the Israelites out of Egypt? With a smile and a tap dance? Believe me, you don't part the Red Sea with some gismo from Korvette's. It takes power.'

'So he's tough, eh?'

'Yes. Very tough. You'd think with all that success he'd be a lot sweeter.'

'How come you know so much?'

'Because we're the chosen people. He takes best care of us of all His children, which I'd also like to someday discuss with Him.'

'What do you pay Him for being chosen?'

'Don't ask.'

So that's how it was. The Jews were into God for a lot. It was the old protection racket. Take care of them in return for a price. And from the way Rabbi Wiseman was talking, He soaked them plenty.

I got into a cab and made it over to Danny's Billiards on Tenth Avenue. The manager was a slimy guy I didn't like.

'Chicago Phil here?'

'Who wants to know?'

I grabbed him by the lapels and took some skin at the same time.

'What, punk?'

'In the back,' he said, with a change of attitude.

Chicago Phil. Forger, bank robber, strong-arm man, and avowed atheist.

'The guy never existed, Kaiser. This is the straight dope. It's a big hype. There's no Mr Big. It's a syndicate. Mostly Sicilian. It's international. But there is no actual head. Except maybe the Pope.'

'I want to meet the Pope.'

'It can be arranged,' he said, winking.

'Does the name Claire Rosensweig mean anything to you?'

'No.'

'Heather Butkiss?'

'Oh, wait a minute. Sure. She's that peroxide job with the bazooms from Radcliffe.'

'Radcliffe? She told me Vassar.'

'Well, she's lying. She's a teacher at Radcliffe. She was mixed up with a philosopher for a while.'

'Pantheist?'

'No. Empiricist, as I remember. Bad guy. Completely rejected Hegel or any dialectical methodology.'

'One of those.'

'Yeah. He used to be a drummer with a jazz trio. Then he got hooked on Logical Positivism. When that didn't work, he tried Pragmatism. Last I heard he stole a lot of money to take a course in Schopenhauer at Columbia. The mob would like to find him — or get their hands on his textbooks so they can resell them.'

'Thanks, Phil.'

'Take it from me, Kaiser. There's no one out there. It's a void. I couldn't pass all those bad checks or screw society the way I do if for one second I was able to recognize any authentic sense of Being. The universe is strictly phenomenological. Nothing's eternal. It's all meaningless.'

'Who won the fifth at Aqueduct?'

'Santa Baby.'

I had a beer at O'Rourke's and tried to add it all up, but it made no sense at all. Socrates was a suicide — or so they said. Christ was murdered. Nietzsche went nuts. If there was someone out there, He sure as hell didn't want anybody to know it. And why was Claire Rosensweig lying about Vassar? Could Descartes have been right? Was the universe dualistic? Or did Kant hit it on the head when he postulated the existence of God on moral grounds?

That night I had dinner with Claire. Ten minutes after the check came, we were in the sack, and, brother, you can have your Western thought. She went through the kind of gymnastics that would have won first prize in the Tia Juana Olympics. After, she lay on the pillow next to me, her long blonde hair sprawling. Our naked bodies still intertwined. I was smoking and staring at the ceiling.

'Claire, what if Kierkegaard's right?'

'You mean?'

'If you can never really *know*. Only have faith.'

'That's absurd.'

'Don't be so rational.'

'Nobody's being rational, Kaiser.' She lit a cigarette. 'Just don't get ontological. Not now. I couldn't bear it if you were ontological with me.'

She was upset. I leaned over and kissed her, and the phone rang. She got it.

'It's for you.'

The voice on the other end was Sergeant Reed of Homicide.

'You still looking for God?'

'Yeah.'

'An all-powerful Being? Great Oneness, Creator of the Universe? First Cause of All Things?'

'That's right.'

'Somebody with that description just showed up at the morgue. You better get down here right away.'

It was Him all right, and from the looks of Him it was a professional job.

'He was dead when they brought Him in.'

'Where'd you find Him?'

'A warehouse on Delancey Street.'

'Any clues?'

'It's the work of an existentialist. We're sure of that.'

'How can you tell?'

'Haphazard way how it was done. Doesn't seem to be any system followed. Impulse.'

'A crime of passion?'

'You got it. Which means you're a suspect, Kaiser.'

'Why me?'

'Everybody down at headquarters knows how you feel about Jaspers.'

'That doesn't make me a killer.'

'Not yet, but you're a suspect.'

Outside on the street I sucked air into my lungs and tried to clear my head. I took a cab over to Newark and got out and walked a block to Giordino's Italian Restaurant. There, at a back table, was His Holiness. It was the Pope, all right. Sitting with two guys I had seen in half a dozen police line-ups.

'Sit down,' he said, looking up from his fettucine. He held out a ring. I gave him my toothiest smile, but didn't kiss it. It bothered him and I was glad. Point for me.

'Would you like some fettucine?'

'No thanks, Holiness. But you go ahead.'

'Nothing? Not even a salad?'

'I just ate.'

'Suit yourself, but they make a great Roquefort dressing here. Not like at the Vatican, where you can't get a decent meal.'

'I'll come right to the point, Pontiff. I'm looking for God.'

'You came to the right person.'

'Then He does exist?' They all found this very amusing and laughed. The hood next to me said, 'Oh, that's funny. Bright boy wants to know if He exists.'

I shifted my chair to get comfortable and brought the leg down on his little toe. 'Sorry.' But he was steaming.

'Sure He exists, Lupowitz, but I'm the only one that communicates with him. He speaks only through me.'

'Why you pal?'

'Because I got the red suit.'

'This get-up?'

'Don't knock it. Every morning I rise, put on this red suit, and suddenly I'm a big cheese. It's all in the suit. I mean, face it, if I went around in slacks and a sports jacket, I couldn't get arrested religion-wise.'

'Then it's a hype. There's no God.'

'I don't know. But what's the difference? The money's good.'

'You ever worry the laundry won't get your red suit back on time and you'll be like the rest of us?'

'I use the special one-day service. I figure it's worth the extra few cents to be safe.'

'Name Claire Rosensweig mean anything to you?'

'Sure. She's in the science department at Bryn Mawr.'

'Science, you say? Thanks.'

'For what?'

'The answer, Pontiff.' I grabbed a cab and shot over the George Washington Bridge. On the way I stopped at my office and did some fast checking. Driving to Claire's apartment, I put the pieces together, and for the first time they fit. When I got there she was in a diaphanous peignoir and something seemed to be troubling her.

'God is dead. The police were here. They're looking for you. They think an existentialist did it.'

'No, sugar. It was you.'

'What? Don't make jokes, Kaiser.'

'It was you that did it.'

'What are you saying?'

'You, baby. Not Heather Butkiss or Claire Rosensweig, but Doctor Ellen Shepherd.'

'How did you know my name?'

'Professor of physics at Bryn Mawr. The youngest one ever to head a department there. At the mid-winter Hop you get stuck on a jazz musician who's heavily into philosophy. He's married, but that doesn't stop you. A couple of nights in the hay and it feels like love. But it doesn't work out because something comes between you. God. Y'see, sugar, he believed, or wanted to, but you, with your pretty little scientific mind, had to have absolute certainty.'

'No, Kaiser, I swear.'

'So you pretend to study philosophy because that gives you a chance to eliminate certain obstacles. You get rid of Socrates easy enough, but Descartes takes over, so you use Spinoza to get rid of Descartes, but when Kant doesn't come through you have to get rid ot him too.'

'You don't know what you're saying.'

'You made mincemeat out of Leibniz, but that wasn't good enough for you because you knew if anybody believed Pascal you were dead, so he had to be gotten rid of too, but that's where you made your mistake because you trusted Martin Buber. Except, sugar, he was soft. He believed in God, so you had to get rid of God yourself.'

'Kaiser, you're mad!'

'No, baby. You posed as a pantheist and that gave you access to Him — *if* He existed, which he did. He went with you to Shelby's party and when Jason wasn't looking, you killed Him.'

'Who the hell are Shelby and Jason?'

'What's the difference. Life's absurd now anyway.'

'Kaiser,' she said, suddenly trembling. 'You wouldn't turn me in?'

'Oh yes, baby. When the Supreme Being gets knocked off, *somebody's* got to take the rap.'

'Oh, Kaiser, we could go away together. Just the two of us. We could forget about philosophy. Settle down and maybe get into semantics.'

'Sorry, sugar. It's no dice.'

She was all tears now as she started lowering the shoulder straps of her peignoir and I was standing there suddenly with a naked Venus whose whole body seemed to be saying, Take me — I'm yours. A Venus whose right hand tousled my hair while her left hand had picked up a forty-five and was holding it behind my back. I let go with a slug from my thirty-eight before she could pull the trigger, and she dropped her gun and doubled over in disbelief.

'How could you, Kaiser?'

She was fading fast, but I managed to get it in, in time.

'The manifestation of the universe as a complex idea unto itself as opposed to being in or outside the true Being of itself is inherently a conceptual nothingness or Nothingness in relation to any abstract form of existing or to exist or having existed in perpetuity and not subject to laws of physicality or motion or ideas relating to non-matter or the lack of objective Being or subjective otherness.'

It was a subtle concept but I think she understood before she died.

From My Philosophy

Eternal nothingness is O.K. if you're dressed for it.

If only Dionysus were alive! Where would he eat?

Not only is there no God, but try getting a plumber on weekends.

Richard Harris Barham (1788–1845)

Sir Rupert the Fearless, A Legend of Germany

From The Ingoldsby Legends

Sir Rupert the Fearless, a gallant young knight,
Was equally ready to tipple or fight,
   Crack a crown, or a bottle,   Cut sirloin, or throttle;
In brief, or as Hume says, 'to sum up the tottle,'
Unstain'd by dishonour, unsullied by fear,
All his neighbours pronounced him a *preux chevalier*.
Despite these perfections, corporeal and mental,
He had one slight defect, viz. a rather lean rental;
Besides, as 'tis own'd there are spots in the sun,
So it must be confessed that Sir Rupert had one;
   Being rather unthinking,   He'd scarce sleep a wink in
A night, but addict himself sadly to drinking,
   And, what moralists say   Is as naughty — to play,
To *Rouge et Noir*, Hazard, Short Whist, Escarté;
Till these and a few less defensible fancies
Brought the Knight to the end of his slender finances.

   When at length through his boozing,
   And tenants refusing
Their rents, swearing 'times were so bad they were losing,'
   His steward said, 'O, sir.   It's some time ago, sir,
Since aught through my hands reach'd the baker or grocer,
And the tradesmen in general are grown great complainers,'
Sir Rupert the brave thus addressed his retainers:

   'My friends, since the stock   Of my father's old hock
Is out, with the Kürchwasser, Barsac, Moselle,
And we're fairly reduced to the pump and the well,
   I presume to suggest,   We shall all find it best
For each to shake hands with his friends ere he goes,
Mount his horse, if he has one, and — follow his nose;
   As to me, I opine,   Left *sans* money or wine,
My best way is to throw myself into the Rhine,
Where pitying travellers may sigh, as they cross over,
   "Though he lived a *roué*, yet he died a philosopher."'

The Knight, having bow'd out his friends thus politely,
Got into his skiff, the full moon shining brightly,
   By the light of whose beam,
   He soon spied on the stream
A dame, whose complexion was fair as new cream,
   Pretty pink silken hose   Cover'd ankles and toes,
In other respects she was scanty of clothes;
For, so says tradition, both written and oral,
Her *one* garment was loop'd up with bunches of coral.
Full sweetly she sang to a sparkling guitar,
With silver cords stretch'd over Derbyshire spar,
   And she smiled on the Knight,
   Who, amazed at the sight,
Soon found his astonishment merged in delight;
   But the stream by degrees
   Now rose up to her knees,
Till at length it invaded her very chemise,
While the heavenly strain, as the wave seemed to swallow her,
And slowly she sank, sounded fainter and hollower;
   —Jumping up in his boat,   And discarding his coat,
'Here goes,' cried Sir Rupert, 'by Jingo I'll follow her!'
Then into the water he plunged with a souse
That was heard quite distinctly by those in the house.

Down, down, forty fathom and more from the brink,
Sir Rupert the Fearless continues to sink,
   And, as downward he goes,
   Still the cold water flows
Through his ears, and his eyes, and his mouth, and his nose,
Till the rum and the brandy he'd swallow'd since lunch
Wanted nothing but lemon to fill him with punch;
Some minutes elapsed since he enter'd the flood
Ere his heels touch'd the bottom, and stuck in the mud.

   But oh! what a sight   Met the eyes of the Knight,
When he stood in the depth of the stream bolt upright!–
   A grand stalactite hall,   Like the cave of Fingal,
Rose above and about him; — great fishes and small
Came thronging around him, regardless of danger,
And seemed all agog for a peep at the stranger.
Their figures and forms to describe, language fails —
They'd such very odd heads, and such very odd tails;

Of their genus or species a sample to gain,
You would ransack all Hungerford market in vain;
   E'en the famed Mr Myers
   Would scarcely find buyers,
Though hundreds of passengers doubtless would stop
To stare, were such monsters expos'd in his shop.

But little reck'd Rupert these queer-looking brutes,
  Or the efts and the newts   That crawled up his boots,
For a sight, beyond any of which I've made mention,
In a moment completely absorb'd his attention.
A huge crystal bath, which, with water far clearer
Than George Robins' filters, or Thorpe's (which are dearer),
   Have ever distill'd,   To the summit was fill'd;
Lay stretch'd out before him, — and every nerve thrill'd
   As scores of young women
   Were diving and swimming,
Till the vision a perfect quandary put him in; —
All slightly accoutred in gauzes and lawns,
They came floating about him like so many prawns.

Sir Rupert, who (barring the few peccadilloes
Alluded to) ere he leapt into the billows
Possess'd irreproachable morals, began
To feel rather queer, as a modest young man;
When forth stepp'd a dame, whom he recognised soon
As the one he had seen by the light of the moon,
And lisp'd, while a soft smile attended each sentence,
'Sir Rupert, I'm happy to make your acquaintance;
   My name is Lurline,   And the ladies you've seen,
All do me the honour to call me their Queen;
I'm delighted to see you, sir, down in the Rhine here,
And hope you can make it convenient to dine here.'

   The Knight blush'd, and bowed,
   As he ogled the crowd
Of subaqueous beauties, then answer'd aloud:
'Ma'am, you do me much honour, — I cannot express
The delight I shall feel — if you'll pardon my dress —
May I venture to say, when a gentleman jumps
In the river at midnight for want of "the dumps,"
He rarely puts on his knee-breeches and pumps;

If I could but have guess'd — what I sensibly feel —
Your politeness — I'd not have come *en dishabille*,
But have put on my *silk* tights in lieu of my *steel*.'

Quoth the lady, 'Dear sir, no apologies, pray,
You will take out "pot-luck" in the family way;
    We can give you a dish   Of some decentish fish,
And our water's thought fairish; but here in the Rhine,
I can't say we pique ourselves much on our wine.'

The Knight made a bow more profound than before,
When a Dory-faced page oped the dining-room door,
    And said, bending his knee,   *'Madame, on a servi!'*
Rupert tender'd his arm, led Lurline to her place,
And a fat little Mer-man stood up and said grace.

What boots it to tell of the viands, or how she
Apologis'd much for their plain water-souchy,
    Want of Harvey's, and Cross's,
    And Burgess's sauces?
Or how Rupert, on his side, protested, by Jove, he
Preferr'd his fish plain, without soy or anchovy,
    Suffice it the meal   Boasted trout, perch, and eel,
Besides some remarkably fine salmon peel.
The Knight, sooth to say, thought much less of the fishes
Than of what they were served on, the massive gold dishes;
While his eye, as it glanced now and then on the girls,
Was caught by their persons much less than their pearls,
And a thought came across him and caused him to muse,
    'If I could but get hold   Of some of that gold,
I might manage to pay off my rascally Jews!'

When dinner was done, at a sign to the lasses,
The table was clear'd, and they put on fresh glasses;
    Then the lady addressed   Her redoubtable guest
Much as Dido, of old, did the pious Eneas,
'Dear sir, what induced you to come down and see us?' —
Rupert gave her a glance most bewitching and tender,
Loll'd back in his chair, put his toes on the fender,
    And told her outright   How that he, a young Knight,
Had never been last at a feast or a fight;
    But that keeping good cheer   Every day in the year,

And drinking neat wines all the same as small-beer,
  Had exhausted his rent,   And, his money all spent,
How he borrow'd large sums at two hundred per cent;
  How they follow'd — and then,
  The once civillest of men,
Messrs Howard and Gibbs, made him bitterly rue it he
'd ever raised money by way of annuity;
And, his mortgages being about to foreclose,
How he jump'd in the river to finish his woes!

Lurline was affected, and own'd, with a tear,
That a story so mournful had ne'er met her ear;
  Rupert, hearing her sigh,   Look'd uncommonly sly,
And said, with some emphasis, 'Ah! miss, had I
  A few pounds of those metals
  You waste here on kettles,
  Then, Lord once again   Of my spacious domain,
A free Count of the Empire once more I might reign,
  With Lurline at my side,   My adorable bride
(For the parson should come, and the knot should be tied);
No couple so happy on earth should be seen
As Sir Rupert the brave and his charming Lurline;
Not that money's my object — No, hang it! I scorn it —
And as for my rank — but that *you'd* so adorn it —
  I'd abandon it all   To remain your true thrall,
And, instead of "the *Great*," be call'd "Rupert the *Small*";
— To gain but your smiles, were I sardanapalus,
I'd descend from my throne, and be boots at an ale-house.'[1]

  Lurline hung her head,   Turned pale, and then red,
Growing faint at this sudden proposal to wed,
As though his abruptness, in 'popping the question'
So soon after dinner, disturb'd her digestion.
  Then, averting her eye,   With a lover-like sigh,
'You are welcome,' she murmur'd, in tones most bewitching,
'To every utensil I have in my kitchen!'
  Upstarted the Knight,   Half mad with delight,
  Round her finely-form'd waist
  He immediately placed
One arm, which the lady most closely embraced,

[1]'Sardanapalus' and 'Boots,' the Zenith and Nadir of human society.

Of her lily-white fingers the other made capture,
And he press'd his adored to his bosom with rapture.
'And, oh!' he exclaim'd, 'let them go catch my skiff, I
'll be home in a twinkling, and back in a jiffy,
Nor one moment procrastinate longer my journey
Than to put up the banns and kick out the attorney.'

One kiss to her lip, and one squeeze to her hand,
And Sir Rupert already was half-way to land,
 For a sour-visaged Triton,
 With features would frighten
Old Nick, caught him up in one hand, though no light one,
Sprang up through the waves, popp'd him into his funny,
Which some others already had half-fill'd with money;
In fact, 'twas so heavily laden with ore
And pearls, 'twas a mercy he got it to shore;
 But Sir Rupert was strong, And, while pulling along,
Still he heard, faintly sounding, the water-nymphs' song.

Lady of the Naiads

 'Away! away! to the mountain's brow,
  Where the castle is darkly frowning;
 And the vassals, all in goodly row,
  Weep for their lord a-drowning!
 Away! away! to the steward's room,
  Where law with its wig and robe is;
 Throw us out John Doe and Richard Roe,
  And sweetly we'll tickle their tobies!'

The unearthly voices scarce had ceased their yelling,
When Rupert reach'd his old baronial dwelling.

 What rejoicing was there!
 How the vassals did stare!
The old housekeeper put a clean shirt down to air,
 For she saw by her lamp
 That her master's was damp,
And she fear'd he'd catch cold, and lumbago and cramp;
But, scorning what she did, The Knight never heeded
Wet jacket or trousers, nor thought of repining,

Since their pockets had got such a delicate lining.
   But oh! what dismay   Fill'd the tribe of *Ca Sa*,
When they found he'd the cash, and intended to pay!
Away went '*cognovits*,' 'bills,' 'bonds,' and 'escheats,'—
Rupert clear'd off all scores, and took proper receipts.

   Now no more he sends out
   For pots of brown stout
Or *schnaps*, but resolves to do henceforth without,
Abjure from this hour all excess and ebriety,
Enrol himself one of a Temp'rance Society,
   All riot eschew,   Begin life anew,
And new-cushion and hassock the family pew!
Nay, to strengthen him more in his new mode of life
He boldly determines to take him a wife.

Now, many would think that the Knight, from a nice sense
Of honour, should put Lurline's name in the licence,
And that, for a man of his breeding and quality,
   To break faith and troth.   Confirm'd by an oath,
Is not quite consistent with rigid morality;
But whether the nymph was forgot, or he thought her
From her essence scarce wife, but at best wife-and-water,
   And declined as unsuited,   A bride so diluted—
   Be this as it may,   He, I'm sorry to say
(For, all things considered, I own 'twas a rum thing),
Made proposals in form to Miss *Una Von*—something
(Her name has escaped me), sole heiress, and niece
To a highly respectable Justice of Peace.

   'Thrice happy's the wooing   That's not long a-doing!'
So much time is saved in the billing and cooing—
The ring is now bought, the white favours, and gloves,
And all the *et cetera* which crown people's loves;
A magnificent bride-cake comes home from the baker,
And lastly appears, from the German Long Acre,
That shaft which the sharpest in all Cupid's quiver is,
A plum-colour'd coach, and rich Pompadour liveries.

   'Twas a comely sight   To behold the Knight,
With his beautiful bride, dress'd all in white,
And the bridesmaids fair with their long lace veils,

As they all walk'd up to the altar rails,
While nice little boys, the incense dispensers,
March'd in front with white surplices, bands, and gilt censers.

With a gracious air, and a smiling look,
Mess John had open'd his awful book,
And had read so far as to ask if to wed he meant?
And if 'he knew any just cause or impediment?'
When from base to turret the castle shook!!!
Then came a sound of a mighty rain
Dashing against each storeyed pane,
The wind blew loud,　And a coal-black cloud
O'ershadowed the church, and the party, and crowd;
How it could happen they could not divine
The morning had been so remarkably fine!

Still the darkness increased, till it reach'd such a pass
That the sextoness hasten'd to turn on the gas;
　But harder it pour'd,　And the thunder roar'd,
As if heaven and earth were coming together;
None ever had witness'd such terrible weather.
　Now louder it crash'd,　And the lightning flash'd,
　Exciting the fears　Of the sweet little dears
In the veils, as it danced on the brass chandeliers;
The parson ran off, though a stout-hearted Saxon,
When he found that a flash had set fire to his caxon.

Though all the rest trembled, as might be expected,
Sir Rupert was perfectly cool and collected,
　And endeavoured to cheer　His bride, in her ear
Whisp'ring tenderly, 'Pray don't be frighten'd, my dear;
Should it even set fire to the castle, and burn it, you're
Amply insured, both for buildings and furniture.'
　But now, from without　A trustworthy scout
　Rush'd hurriedly in　Wet through to the skin,
Informing his master 'the river was rising,
And flooding the grounds in a way quite surprising.'

He'd no time to say more,　For already the roar
Of the waters was heard as they reach'd the church door,
While, high on the first wave that roll'd in, was seen,
Riding proudly, the form of the angry Lurline;

And all might observe, by her glance fierce and stormy,
She was stung by the *spretae injuria formae*.

What she said to the Knight, what she said to the bride,
What she said to the ladies who stood by her side,
What she said to the nice little boys in white clothes,
Oh, nobody mentions, — for nobody knows;
For the roof tumbled in, and the walls tumbled out,
And the folks tumbled down, all confusion and rout,
 The rain kept on pouring,
 The flood kept on roaring,
The billows and water-nymphs roll'd more and more in;
 Ere the close of the day
All was clean washed away—
One only survived who could hand down the news,
A little old woman that open'd the pews;
 She was born off, but stuck,
 By the greatest good luck,
In an oak-tree, and there she hung, crying and screaming,
And saw all the rest swallow'd up the wild stream in;
 In vain all the week,   Did the fishermen seek
For the bodies, and poke in each cranny and creek;
 In vain was their search
 After ought in the church,
They caught nothing but weeds, and perhaps a few perch;

 The Humane Society   Tried a variety
Of methods, and brought down, to drag for the wreck, tackles,
But they only fish'd up the clerk's tortoise-shell spectacles.

Moral

This tale has a moral   Ye youths, oh, beware
Of liquor, and how you run after the fair!
Shun playing at *shorts* — avoid quarrels and jars—
And don't take to smoking those nasty cigars!
— Let no run of bad luck, or despair for some Jewess-eyed
Damsel, induce you to contemplate suicide!
Don't sit up much later than ten or eleven!—
Be up in the morning by half after seven!

Keep from flirting — nor risk, warned by Rupert's miscarriage,
An action for breach of a promise of marriage;—
   Don't fancy old fishes! Don't prig silver dishes!
And to sum up the whole, in the shortest phrase I know,
BEWARE OF THE RHINE, AND TAKE CARE OF THE RHINO!

Beachcomber (J. B. Morton) (1893–1979)
Stalemate

(When the curtain rises, the stage is in darkness. The OLD MAN, aged ninety-six, is groaning in one corner of the stage, and the OLD WOMAN, aged ninety-eight, is groaning in the other corner. The auditorium is in darkness, too. But after half an hour of this the darkness melts, and dawn breaks. All the birds are singing out of tune — for instance, a thrush is croaking like a frog. The OLD MAN is discovered lying on the seashore, gnawing a large rock, while the OLD WOMAN is half-buried in the sand, and is a good deal bothered by seagulls. As this is expressionism, the OLD MAN symbolises the Futility of Life, and the OLD WOMAN represents the Hopelessness of Everything. The seagulls are the awful thoughts that trouble us in the night.)

OLD MAN: (*lugubriously*): Twelve hundred and forty-three.

OLD WOMAN: (*eagerly*): Yes? —

(*Silence*)

OLD MAN: Twelve hundred and forty-four.

OLD WOMAN: What do you mean?

OLD MAN: (*biting rock savagely*): Twelve hundred and forty-five! Twelve hundred and forty-five times I have bitten this rock, without any result, save only injury to the teeth.

OLD WOMAN: Our masters are very cruel.

OLD MAN: Very cruel.

OLD WOMAN: They do not realise.

OLD MAN: No.

OLD WOMAN: But if they did realise —

OLD MAN: Ah then!

OLD WOMAN: The seagulls are troublesome.

OLD MAN: Life is nothing but seagulls.

(*A clergyman with a wheelbarrow passes slowly across the stage*)

OLD WOMAN:	(*blowing sand from her clothes*): Our son! Where can he be?
OLD MAN:	The seagulls.
OLD WOMAN:	Ah, the seagulls!

(*Another clergyman with another wheelbarrow passes slowly across the stage*)

OLD MAN:	There, there!
OLD WOMAN:	What was it the Controller said?

(*Darkness falls again*)

(*When the curtain rises the OLD MAN is still gnawing the rock, and the OLD WOMAN is still blowing sand off her clothes. In the sky there is a curious brown moon with violet stripes, and a number of scarlet and blue stars*)

OLD MAN: (*biting the rock*): Four thousand seven hundred and thirty-two, four thousand seven hundred and thirty-three, four thousand seven hundred and thirty-four —

(*A long silence, broken only by the screams of seagulls committing suicide on the rocky shore*)

OLD WOMAN:	(*blowing sand*): Shall I never be free from it?
OLD MAN:	Not till I have finished this rock. Four thousand seven hundred and thir—

(*A young man falls from the clifftop into the sea and is drowned*)

OLD MAN: –ty-five, four thousand seven hundred and thir—

(*An old man falls from the clifftop into the sea and is drowned*)

OLD MAN:	–ty-six, four thou—
OLD WOMAN:	That was my brother.

(Enter a mad VETERINARY SURGEON pursued by a NAVAL ARCHITECT)

NAVAL ARCHITECT: Which way did he go?
VET. *(to OLD MAN)*: I am your grandfather.
OLD MAN: Of course. Will you have some rock?
NAVAL ARCHITECT: What does it all mean?

(Darkness falls, a giraffe wanders across the stage, and nothing is heard but the teeth of the OLD MAN grating on the rock, and the sound of the OLD WOMAN blowing sand off her clothes)

(Twilight. The birds are still singing out of tune, and the body of the NAVAL ARCHITECT is hanging from a bit of scenery. The giraffe lies in a stupor. The OLD WOMAN, rather breathless, is still trying to blow sand from her clothes. The surviving seagulls are too ill and tired to fly, and are squatting on a rock. The OLD MAN still gnaws away)

OLD MAN: *(biting the rock methodically)*: Twenty-six thousand four hundred and ninety-five, twenty-six thousand four hundred and ninety-six, twenty-six thousand four hundred and ninety-seven.
OLD WOMAN: Whoof!

(A seagull dies)

OLD MAN: It was eighty-one years ago.
OLD WOMAN: I remember.

(Six piano-tuners are drowned within sight of the shore)

OLD MAN: The dawn is coming.
OLD WOMAN: It is dusk.
OLD MAN: Dawn and dusk are only two aspects of the same thing. What is black to one-half of the world is white to the other. Nothing begins and nothing ends. Life is a flux and

counterflux. Our being is both future and past. There is no present.

(*A cough is heard*)

OLD WOMAN: What was that?
OLD MAN: The music of eternity.

(*The curtain descends slowly, as the OLD MAN hangs himself to a rock by his frayed braces, which break and precipitate him into the sea. The OLD WOMAN lies down in the sand. The seagulls die. The cough is repeated and FATE enters, grinning.*)

A Folk Song

As oi wur a-waalkin' boi Bolzover Green
  (Wi' a dumbledown junket an' dumbledown dee),
Oi zaw as wot oi never 'ad zeen
  (An' a fermitty pudden vor paarson).

'Moi lass,' zes oi, oi zes, zes oi
  (Wi' a dumbledown junket an' dumbledown dee),
''Tain't no accord fer yew tu croi.'
  (An' a fermitty pudden vor paarson).

'Nay, zir,' quoth 'er, 'Nay, zir, oi begs'
  (Wi' a dumbledown junket an' dumbledown dee),
An' off she scuds on 'er two purty legs,
  (An' a fermitty pudden vor paarson).

Zo yew strong lads a luvs good ale
  (Wi' a dumbledown junket an' dumbledown dee),
Yew naow 'ave 'eerd moi deedly tale,
  (An' fermitty pudden vor paarson).

Labour-Saving

The recent International Exhibition of Inventions had among its exhibits 'a collapsible clothes-airer in which a lamp can be put — the invention of a Somerset clergyman'.

Dr Strabismus (Whom God Preserve), of Utrecht, allowed several of his own recent inventions to be shown. Among these interesting exhibits were to be found:

1. A large marmalade-dish which folds up into the shape of a candle-stick.
2. A wooden sausage which, when reversed, pours out a stream of salad-oil into a bowl, in readiness for mixing the salad.
3. An iron cocktail-shaker which, when hit with great strength, rings the front-door bell and returns the cherry.
4. A thick cut-glass walking-stick filled with very small flannel shirts.
5. A large bucket, open at one end to admit bearer.
6. A rubber wheelbarrow for wiping out illuminated addresses.
7. A dummy filter which can be used as a hat-rack or birdcage.
8. A long-distance bacon-pan, in which bacon can be cooked slowly in a greenhouse.
9. A canvas tomato to balance on a trouser-press (for jugglers, principally).
10. A concrete combined sieve and potato-masher.
11. A receptacle for collecting lamp-iron after earthquakes.
12. A musical ballot-box for wet elections, which, simultaneously, fills bottles with bilberries.

The Case of the Twelve Red-Bearded Dwarfs

Another ludicrous scene occurred while Mr Tinklebury Snapdriver,
for the prosecution, was cross-examining Mrs Tasker.

MR SNAPDRIVER:	Your name is Rhoda Tasker?
MRS TASKER:	Obviously, or I wouldn't be here.
MR SNAPDRIVER:	I put it to you that you were once known as Rough-House Rhoda?
MR HERMITAGE:	No, m'lud, Rough-House Rhoda is another lady, who I propose to call — a Mrs Rhoda Mortiboy.
COCKLECARROT:	What a queer name.
A DWARF:	You are speaking of my mother. (*sensation*)
COCKLECARROT:	Is your name Mortiboy?
THE DWARF:	No. Towler's my name.
COCKLECARROT:	(*burying his head in his hands*): I suppose she married again.

THE DWARF:	What do you mean — again? Her name has always been Towler.
COCKLECARROT:	(*groaning*): Mr Hermitage, what is all this about?
MR HERMITAGE:	M'lud, there is a third Rhoda, a Mrs Rhoda Clandon.
COCKLECARROT:	(*to the dwarf, sarcastically*): Is she your mother, too?
THE DWARF:	Yes. My name's Clandon.
COCKLECARROT:	I think, Mr Snapdriver, we had better proceed without this Rhoda business. My nerves won't stand it.
MR SNAPDRIVER:	My next witness is the artiste known as Lucinda — a Mrs Whiting (*everybody looks at the Dwarf*)
COCKLECARROT:	(*with heavy sarcasm*): And, of course —
THE DWARF:	Yes, she is my mother.
COCKLECARROT:	(*roaring*): Then what is your name, you oaf?
THE DWARF:	Charlie Bread. (*Laughter and jeers.*)
COCKLECARROT:	Clear the court! This foolery is intolerable. It will ruin my political career.
MR SNAPDRIVER:	Now, Mrs Tasker, you do not deny that on several occasions you drove these dwarfs, a dozen of them, into Mrs Renton's hall.
MRS TASKER:	That is so.
MR SNAPDRIVER:	What was your motive?
MRS TASKER:	I wanted to drive the dwarfs into her hall.
MR SNAPDRIVER:	But why? Can you give me any reason? You will admit it is an unusual occupation.
MRS TASKER:	Not for me. I've done it all my life.
MR SNAPDRIVER:	You have driven dwarfs into other ladies' houses?
MRS TASKER:	Certainly.
COCKLECARROT:	Where do you get your supply of dwarfs?
MRS TASKER:	From an agency, Fudlow and Trivett.
COCKLECARROT:	Extraordinary. Most extraordinary.
MR HERMITAGE:	Now Dr Spunton, is there, to your knowledge, any disease which could account for Mrs Tasker's strange habits?
DR SPUNTON:	There is. It is called rufo-nanitis. The spymptoms.
MR HERMITAGE:	Symptoms.

DR SPUNTON:	Yes, spymptoms, but I always put a 'p' before a 'y'.
COCKLECARROT:	With what object, might we ask?
DR SPUNTON:	I can't help it, m'lud.
COCKLECARROT:	Do you say pyesterday?
DR SPUNTON:	Pyes, unfortunatelpy. It's hereditarpy. Mpy familpy all do it.
COCKLECARROT:	But why 'p'?
DR SPUNTON:	No, py, m'lud.
COCKLECARROT:	This case is the most preposterous I ever heard. We get nowhere. The evidence is drivel, the whole thing is a travesty of justice. In two weeks we have done nothing but listen to a lot of nonsense. The case will be adjourned until we can clear things up a bit.
DR SPUNTON:	But I was brought all the wapy from Pyelverton.
COCKLECARROT:	Well, go pyack to Pyelverton. Good-pye, and a phappy pjournepy. Pshaw!

The dwarfs were cross-examined today. At least, one of them was cross-examined.

MR HERMITAGE:	Your name is Howard Brassington?
THE DWARF:	(*in a deep, loud voice*): It is no such thing.
MR HERMITAGE:	(*consulting his notes*): What is your name, then?
THE DWARF:	Stanislas George Romney Barlow Barlow Orchmeynders.
MR HERMITAGE:	Two Barlows?
THE DWARF:	Why not?
MR HERMITAGE:	You are a night watchman.
THE DWARF:	Why not?
COCKLECARROT:	Mr Porchminder, you will please answer yes or no.
THE DWARF:	No.
MR HERMITAGE:	Where were you on the night of 10th April?
THE DWARF:	No.
COCKLECARROT:	(*to counsel*): Apart from retaining fees, would it not be better to speed up this case a bit?
THE DWARF:	Yes.

COCKLECARROT:	Send him away. Call Mrs Renton.
MR HERMITAGE:	Speak your mind, Mrs Renton, speak your mind.
MRS RENTON:	I will. I accused Mrs Tasker of driving a dozen red-bearded dwarfs into my hall. She admits she did it. The dwarfs say she did it. Well, what more is there to be said? What are we waiting for?
COCKLECARROT:	Mrs Renton, you do not understand that certain formalities — er — the Law has its own way of doing things.
MRS RENTON:	And that is why I have to come here day after day to listen to all this irrelevant foolery — speeches about the Navy, arguments about a dwarf's mother, fuss about dates, and so on.
COCKLECARROT:	I am the first to admit that there have been irregularities and delays in this case, but —

(*A dwarf shouts loudly, 'M'lud! M'Lud!' COCKLECARROT and MRS RENTON exchange glances*)

MR HERMITAGE:	Well?
THE DWARF:	I think I'm going to be sick.
MRS RENTON:	That is about the only thing that hasn't happened in this case so far.
COCKLECARROT:	Usher, remove that dwarf. The time has, I think, come for you, ladies and gentlemen of the jury, to consider this case on its merits.
FOREMAN OF JURY:	And what, sir, would you say were its merits?
COCKLECARROT:	What would you?
FOREMAN:	We have not so far understood one word of the proceedings.
COCKLECARROT:	I must say there have been moments when I myself seemed to have lost touch with the real world. Nevertheless, certain facts stand out.
FOREMAN	For instance?
COCKLECARROT:	I will not be cross-examined by my own

	jury. You are here to deliver a verdict, not to question me. You have heard the evidence.
FOREMAN:	Was that the evidence? All that horseplay?
COCKLECARROT:	If this continues I shall discharge the jury, and the case will be heard all over again with a new jury. Stop those dwarfs singing! This is not a music hall.

Max Beerbohm (1872–1956)

A Note on the Einstein Theory

From Mainly on Air

It is said that there are, besides Dr Einstein himself, only two men who can claim to have grasped the Theory in full. I cannot claim to be either of these. But I do know a good thing when I see it; and here is a thing that is excellent in its kind — romantically excellent in a kind that is itself high. When I think of rays being deflected by gravity, and of parallel lines at long last converging so that there isn't perhaps, after all, any such thing as Infinity, I draw a very deep breath indeed. The attempt to conceive Infinity had always been quite arduous enough for me. But to imagine the absence of it; to feel that perhaps we and all the stars beyond our ken are somehow cosily (though awfully) closed in by curtain curves beyond which is nothing; and to convince myself, by the way, that this exterior is not (in virtue of *being* nothing) something, and therefore . . . but I lose the thread.

Enough that I never lost the thrill. It excites, it charms me to think of elderly great mathematicians of this and that nation packing their portmanteaux whenever there is to be a solar eclipse, and travelling over land and sea to the Lick Observatory, or to some hardly accessible mountain-top in Kamchatka, and there testing, to the best of their power, the soundness, or unsoundness of the tremendous Theory. So far, the weather has not been very favourable to these undertakings. Nature, who is proud and secretive, has opposed many clouds to the batteries of telescopes. But she has had only a partial success, it seems. Some observations have been more or less clearly made, some conclusions more or less clearly drawn. And these more or less clearly point to the likelihood that what Dr Einstein in his humdrum home evolved from his inner consciousness is all delightfully correct.

But is the British public delighted? It gives no sign of being so. Its newspapers did at the first news of Einstein's existence try, very honourably, to excite it about Einstein and even about his work. It would *not* be excited. Strange! The tamest batting of Hertfordshire *v* Australia, the feeblest goal-keeping of Wormwood Scrubbs *v* Hornsey Rise, the lightest word that falls from the lips of the least accomplished negro boxer, are better 'copy' than any challenge to our notion of the Cosmos. This is all the stranger because the public is not careless of other things than Sport. Its passionate interest in archaeology, for instance, rose to boiling-point, only the other day; it could *not* hear too much about the tomb of Tutankhamen, nor tire of debating whether or not the bones of that king might rightly be disturbed. Why never a word as to the disturbance of our belief that parallel lines can nowhere converge? I haven't grudged Tutankhamen the renewal and immense enlargement of the fame he once had. I have but deplored the huge cold shoulder turned on the living Einstein.

Newton, no greater an innovator than he, is popular enough. Everybody knows something about Gravitation — and all about the apple. Perhaps if Newton had not mentioned that apple, he too would be generally ignored. It is a great advantage for a discoverer to have been inspired by some homely little incident. Newton and the apple. Copernicus and the whipping-top. James Watt and the kettle. But Einstein and — ? Poor Einstein!

Men of his magnitude are not avid of popularity? True; but this does not mean that popularity would be disagreeable to them. When the newspapers were trying to make Relativity a household word, I read an account of Einstein, written by one who knew him, and enhanced by a photograph of him. A very human person, I gathered; far from stand-offish; a player of the fiddle; the constant smoker of a large pipe; a genial, though thoughtful, critic of current things. I liked his views on education. Why all this forcing of a child's memory? Memory — a matter of little moment. Let the child be taught a trade. And 'after all,' said Einstein, dismissing tuition, 'the best thing in the world is a happy face.' It was clear from the photograph that his own face was a happy one. But I discerned in it a certain wistfulness, too — the wistfulness of a thoroughly good fellow whose work somehow repels the attention of that good fellow, the average man. My heart went out to him. I wished I could help him. And now, I think, I can. Hark!

Yesterday afternoon I was walking on the coast road from Rapallo to Zoagli when I saw approaching in the distance a man of strenuous gait, and of aspect neither Italian nor English. His brow was bare to the breeze; and as he drew near I perceived the brow to be a fine one; and as he drew nearer still I perceived the face to be a very happy one— with just a hint in it of wistfulness, which, however, vanished at my words. 'Dr Einstein, I presume?' He clapped a cordial hand on my shoulder; he treated me as an old friend, as a brother, and insisted that we should sit together on the low wall that divides the road from the cliff. Presently — after he had praised the sun and the sea, and had expressed an ardent sympathy with Fascismo, and with Socialismo, no less — I said to him, 'Master (if one who is not a disciple may so address you), tell me: What was it that first put you on the track of the tremendous Theory?' He knitted his fine brow, saying that his memory was not a very good one; but after a while he remembered, and spoke to me as follows:

'One winter's evening, after a hard day's work, I was sitting by my fireside — for I have an open fire in the English fashion, not a stove: I like to sit watching the happy faces in the coals — when my eye lighted on the tongs in the fender. Of course it had often lighted on them before; but this time it carried to my brain a message which my brain could not understand. "Here," I mused, "are two perfectly parallel lines. And yet, and yet, they meet at the extreme ends. How is that?" My friend Professor Schultz had promised to drop in and smoke a pipe with me that evening, and when he came I drew his attention to the phenomenon. He knelt down by the fender, pushed his spectacles up on to his forehead, gazed closely, and muttered, "Gott im Himmel — ja!" I asked him — for he is a very ready man — if he had any explanation to offer. He rose from his knees and sat down on a chair heavily, burying his head in his hands. Suddenly he sprang to his feet. "Einstein," he said. "I believe I have it! I believe that the ironworker who made those bars must have heated them red-hot and then bent the ends towards each other." Dear old Schultz! Always so ready! — so shallow! I suppose I ought not to have laughed; but I did; and Schultz went out in some anger. It was dawn when I rose from the fireside. The fire had long ago burnt itself out, and I was stiff with cold. But my mind was all aglow with the basic principles of Relativismus.'

'The world,' I said quietly, 'shall hear of this, Dr Einstein.'

Hilaire Belloc (1870–1953)
From The Bad Child's Book of Beasts *and* More Beasts for Worse Children

The Marmozet

The species Man and Marmozet

Are intimately linked;

The Marmozet survives as yet,

But Men are all extinct.

The Python

A PYTHON I should not advise,—
It needs a doctor for its eyes,
And has the measles yearly.

However, if you feel inclined
To get one (to improve your mind,
And not from fashion merely),
Allow no music near its cage;

And when it flies into a rage
Chastise it, most severely.

I had an aunt in Yucatan
Who bought a Python from a man
    And kept it for a pet.
She died, because she never knew
These simple little rules and few;—

The Snake is living yet.

Robert Benchley (1889–1945)

Go Down, Sweet Jordan

There used to be a time when four Negroes could get together and tear off a little ripe harmony and nobody thought anything of it except that it sounded great. Now, since spirituals have been taken up socially, you have got to know counterpoint and the 'History of the Key of Four Flats' in order really to appreciate them.

What used to be just plain 'Swing Low, Sweet Chariot' in the old brown book of college songs, along with 'Seeing Nellie Home' and 'Clementine', is now a manifestation of the growth of the Chariot Motif from the ancient African tap-dance through the muted eighth note into assonance and dissonance. And over your ears.

Having heard and read so much about the history of the Negro spiritual, I have been moved to look into the matter myself and have unearthed a large block of data which I am going to work into a book, to be called *The Legal Aspects of the Negro Spiritual*. It will take up the little known origins of the spiritual in Africa and bring it right down to the present day, or rather to December 5, when the book will come out (and go in again after seeing its own shadow).

Commentators and experts on the spiritual do not seem to realise that this particular form of harmony comes from the old African 'vegetable-humming,' dating back to the early seventeenth century and perhaps later. 'Vegetable-humming' or *blakawa* was a chant taken part in by certain members of the tribe who wished they were vegetables and who thought that by humming loudly enough (with the tenor carrying the air) the God of the Harvest would turn them into vegetables and they could get their wish. There is no case on record of any one of them ever having been turned into a vegetable, but they kept on humming just the same, and it is in this strange form of religious ecstasy that the spiritual as we know it had its origin.

Let us take, for example, the spiritual, 'Roll Down Jordan, Roll Up de Lord.' This is one of the best songs for our purpose, as it contains the particular harmonic combinations which are also found in the 'vegetable-humming,' that is, C, G-sharp, A, and E, sliding up very wickedly into D-flat, G-natural, B-flat, and E-sharp. In case the G-sharp slips a little too much and gets into H, the singer must open his mouth very wide but stop making sounds altogether.

The first verse to 'Roll Down Jordan, Roll Up de Lord' goes:

Roll down Jordan; roll up de Lord;
Roll down Jordan; roll up de Lord;

> Roll down Jordan; roll up de Lord;
> Roll down Jordan; roll up de Lord!

We then find the whole spirit of the thing changing and the evangelical note so common among Africans creeping into the second verse:

> Roll down de Lord; roll up Jordan;
> Roll down de Lord; roll up Jordan;
> Roll down de Lord; roll up Jordan;
> Roll down de Lord; roll up Jordan;
> Hey-hey!

Thus, you will see, does the modern chant derive from the old wheat-cake dance, which in its turn, derived from Chicago to Elkhart in four hours (baby talk). In this dance we seem to see the native women filing into the market-place in the early morning to offer up their prayer to the God of Corn on the Cob for better and more edible crops ('O God of the Harvest! Give us some corn that we can eat. That last was terrible! Amen'). The dance itself was taken part in by the local virgins and such young men of the tribe as were willing to be seen out with them. They marched once around the market-place beating drums until someone told them to shut up. Then they seated themselves in a semi-circle, facing inward, and rocked back and forth, back and forth. This made some of them sick and they had to be led out. The rest sat there rocking and crooning until they were eighteen years old, at which time they all got up and went home, pretty sore at themselves for having wasted so much time.

We have now seen how the old tribes handled the problem of what to sing and how to prevent people from singing it. The slave trade, bringing these Negroes and their descendants over to America, foisted the problem on the United States. For a long time, owing to the coloured people not knowing that they were developing a national folk song, nothing was done about it. The Negroes just sat around on pieces of corn-pone and tried out various kinds of swipes which they aggravated by the use of the banjo. One of the favourite songs of this era ran thus:

(*Bases*)	M-m-m-m-m-m-m-m-m-m.
(*Tenors*)	M-m-m-m-m-m-m-m-m-m.
(*First tenor solo*)	M-m-m-m-m-m-m-m-m-m.
(*Second tenor solo*)	M-m-m-m-m-m-m-m-m-m.
(*Unison*)	Comin' fer to carry me home.

Under this ran the banjo accompaniment something like this:

> Plunky-plunky-plunky-plunky,
> Plunky-plunky-plunky-plunky,
> Plunky-plunky-plunky-plunky,
> Plunky-plunky-plunky-plunky,
> Plunk!

Here we find for the first time some evidence of the spirit of the whole race stirring in its captivity. We seem to see the women filing into the market-place in the early morning to raise their prayer to the God of the Harvest — I guess that goes with the other song.

Gradually, during the Reconstruction Period following the Civil War, carpetbaggers from the North came in and organised these singing groups into glee-clubs, each with a leader and white gloves. They taught the basses to sing 'Zum-zum-zum-zum' instead of 'M-m-m-m-m-m' and wrote extra verses to many of the numbers to be sung as encores. The coloured people didn't know what to make of all this and many of them stopped singing entirely and went in for tap-dancing. But the popularization of the Negro spiritual was on its way and special writers were assigned to the job of making up words which would sound rather native and yet would tell a story. It was found that only four words were needed for each song, as they were always repeated. Thus we have the growth of such songs as 'Carryin' de Clouds on Jehovah's Back, "Ain't Gwine ter Pray fer de Old Black Roan,' and 'Ramona.' The growth of the narrative in such songs can be traced in the following, entitled 'All God's Fish is A-comin' Home':

> Oh, I went fer ter see de lightnin',
> Oh, I went fer ter see de lightnin',
> Oh, I went fer ter see de lightnin',
>   But de lightnin' warn't ter home.
>
> Oh, I went fer ter see de thunder,
> Oh, I went fer ter see de thunder,
> Oh, I went fer ter see de thunder,
>   But de thunder warn't ter home.
>
> Oh, I went fer ter see de rain (pronounced 'ray-un')
> Oh, I went fer ter see de rain,
> Oh, I went fer ter see de rain,
>   But de rain warn't ter home.

And so on the song goes, with the singer going to see, in rapid succession, the fog, the light mist, the snow, the oysters, the river, Lake Placid, the man about coming to carry away the ashes, and finally the Lord, none of them being at home except the Lord and he was busy.

This marks the final development of the spiritual as a regenerative force and also marks the point at which I give up. I would, however, like to hear four good coloured singers again without having to put my glasses on to follow the libretto.

John Betjeman (1906–   )

Dorset

Rime Intrinsica, Fontmell Magna, Sturminster Newton and Melbury
    Bubb,
Whist upon whist upon whist upon whist drive, in Institute, Legion
    and Social Club,
Horny hands that hold the aces which this morning held the plough—
While Tranter Reuben, T. S. Eliot, H. G. Wells and Edith Sitwell lie in
    Mellstock Churchyard now.

Lord's Day bells from Bingham's Melcombe, Iwerne Minster,
    Shroton, Plush,
Down the grass between the Beeches, mellow in the evening hush.
Gloved the hands that hold the hymn-book, which this morning
    milked the cow—
While Tranter Reuben, Mary Borden, Brian Howard and Harold
    Acton lie in Mellstock Churchyard now.

Light's abode, celestial Salem! Lamps of evening, smelling strong,
Gleaming on the pitch-pine, waiting, almost empty evensong:
From the aisles each window smiles on grave and grass and yew-tree
    bough—
While Tranter Reuben, Gordon Selfridge, Edna Best and Thomas
    Hardy lie in Mellstock Churchyard now.

(Note: The names in the last lines of these stanzas are put in not out of malice or satire but merely for their euphony.)

Niels Mogens Bodecker (1922—   )

House Flies

What makes
common house flies
trying
is
that they keep
multiflieing.

Gyles Brandreth (1948–   )

Ode to My Goldfish

O
Wet
Pet!

Gelett Burgess (1866–1951)

I never saw a Purple Cow,
I never hope to see one;
But I can tell you, anyhow,
I'd rather see than be one.

Ah Yes! I Wrote the 'Purple Cow'
I'm Sorry, now, I Wrote it!
But I can Tell you, Anyhow,
I'll Kill you if you Quote it!

The Proper Way to Leave a Room
Is not to Plunge it into Gloom;
Just Make a Joke before you Go
And then Escape before They Know.

Robert Burns (1759–96)

Tam O'Shanter

When chapman billies leave the street,
And drouthy neibors neibors meet,
As market-days are wearing late,
An' folk begin to tak the gate;
While we sit bousing at the nappy,
An' getting fou and unco happy,
We think na on the lang Scots miles,
The mosses, water, slaps, and styles,
That lie between us and our hame,
Where sits our sulky sullen dame,
Gathering her brows like gathering storm,
Nursing her wrath to keep it warm.

This truth fand honest Tam O'Shanter,
As he frae Ayr ae night did canter—
(Auld Ayr, wham ne'er a town surpasses
For honest men and bonnie lasses).
  O Tam! hadst thou but been sae wise
As ta'en thy ain wife Kate's advice!
She tauld thee weel thou was a skellum,
A bletherin', blusterin', drunken blellum;
That frae November till October,
Ae market-day thou was na sober;
That ilka melder wi' the miller
Thou sat as lang as thou had siller;
That every naig was ca'd a shoe on,
The smith and thee gat roarin' fou on;
That at the Lord's house, even on Sunday,
Thou drank wi' Kirkton Jean till Monday.
She prophesied that, late or soon,
Thou would be found deep drown'd in Doon;
Or catch'd wi' warlocks in the mirk
By Alloway's auld haunted kirk.
  Ah, gentle dames! it gars me greet
To think how mony counsels sweet,
How mony lengthen'd sage advices,
The husband frae the wife despises!
  But to our tale: Ae market night,
Tam had got planted unco right,
Fast by an ingle, bleezing finely,
Wi' reaming swats, that drank divinely;
And at his elbow, Souter Johnny,
His ancient, trusty, drouthy crony;
Tam lo'ed him like a very brither;
They had been fou for weeks thegither.
The night drave on wi' sangs and clatter.
And aye the ale was growing better:
The landlady and Tam grew gracious,
Wi' favours secret, sweet, and precious;
The souter tauld his queerest stories;
The landlord's laugh was ready chorus:
The storm without might rair and rustle,
Tam did na mind the storm a whistle.
  Care, mad to see a man sae happy,
E'en drown'd himsel amang the nappy.

As bees flee hame wi' lades o' treasure,
The minutes wing'd their way wi pleasure;
Kings may be blest, but Tam was glorious,
O'er a' the ills o' life victorious!
    But pleasures are like poppies spread—
You seized the flow'r, its bloom is shed;
Or like the snow falls in the river—
A moment white, then melts for ever;
Or like the borealis race,
That flit ere you can point their place;
Or like the rainbow's lovely form
Evanishing amid the storm.
Nae man can tether time nor tide;
The hour approaches Tam maun ride;
That hour, o' night's black arch the key-stane,
That dreary hour, he mounts his beast in;
And sic a night he taks the road in,
As ne'er poor sinner was abroad in.
    The wind blew as 'twad blawn its last;
The rattling show'rs rose on the blast;
The speedy gleams the darkness swallow'd;
Loud, deep, and lang, the thunder bellow'd:
That night, a child might understand,
The De'il had business on his hand.
    Weel mounted on his gray mare, Meg,
A better never lifted leg,
Tam skelpit on thro' dub and mire,
Despising wind, and rain, and fire;
Whiles holding fast his gude blue bonnet;
Whiles crooning o'er some auld Scots sonnet;
Whiles glow'ring round wi' prudent cares,
Lest bogles catch him unawares.
Kirk-Alloway was drawing nigh,
Whare ghaists and houlets nightly cry,
    By this time he was cross the ford,
Where in the snaw the chapman smoor'd;
And past the birks and meikle stane,
Where drunken Charlie brak's neck-bane;
And thro' the whins, and by the cairn,
Where hunters fand the murder'd bairn;
And near the thorn, aboon the well,
Where Mungo's mither hang'd hersel.

Before him Doon pours all his floods;
The doubling storm roars thro' the woods;
The lightnings flash from pole to pole;
Near and more near the thunders roll:
When, glimmering thro' the groaning trees,
Kirk-Alloway seem'd in a bleeze;
Thro' ilka bore the beams were glancing;
And loud resounded mirth and dancing.
   Inspiring bold John Barleycorn!
What dangers thou canst make us scorn!
Wi' tippenny, we fear nae evil;
Wi' usquebae, we'll face the devil!
The swats sae ream'd in Tammie's noddle,
Fair play, he car'd na deils a boddle!
But Maggie stood right sair astonish'd,
Till, by the heel and hand admonish'd,
She ventur'd forward on the light;
And, vow! Tam saw an unco sight!
Warlocks and witches in a dance!
Nae cotillon brent new frae France.
But hornpipes, jigs, strathspeys, and reels,
Put life and mettle in their heels.
A winnock-bunker in the east,
There sat auld Nick, in shape o' beast—
A touzie tyke, black, grim, and large!
To gie them music was his charge:
He screw'd the pipes and gart them skirl.
Till roof and rafters a' did dirl.
Coffins stood round like open presses,
That shaw'd the dead in their last dresses;
And by some devilish cantraip sleight
Each in its cauld hand held a light,
By which heroic Tam was able
To note upon the haly table
A murderer's banes in gibbet-airns;
Twa span-lang, wee, unchristen'd bairns;
A thief new-cutted frae the rape—
Wi' his last gasp his gab did gape;
Five tomahawks, wi' blude red rusted;
Five scymitars, wi' murder crusted;
A garter, which a babe had strangled;
A knife, a father's throat had mangled,

Whom his ain son o' life bereft—
The gray hairs yet stack to the heft;
Wi' mair of horrible and awfu',
Which even to name wad be unlawfu'.
  As Tammie glowr'd, amaz'd, and curious,
The mirth and fun grew fast and furious:
The piper loud and louder blew;
The dancers quick and quicker flew;
They reel'd, they set, they cross'd, they cleekit,
Till ilka carlin swat and reekit,
And coost her duddies to the wark,
And linkit at it in her sark!
  Now Tam, O Tam! had thae been queans,
A' plump and strapping in their teens;
Their sarks, instead o' creeshie flannen,
Been snaw-white seventeen hunder linen!
Thir breeks o' mine, my only pair,
That ance were plush, o' gude blue hair,
I wad hae gi'en them off my hurdies,
For ae blink o' the bonnie burdies!
  But wither'd beldams, auld and droll,
Rigwoodie hags wad spean a foal,
Louping and flinging on a crummock,
I wonder didna turn thy stomach.
  But Tam kent what was what fu' brawlie
There was ae winsome wench and walie
That night enlisted in the core,
Lang after kent on Carrick shore!
(For mony a beast to dead she shot,
And perish'd mony a bonnie boat,
And shook baith meikle corn and bear.
And kept the country-side in fear.)
Her cutty sark, o' Paisley harn,
That while a lassie she had worn,
In longitude tho' sorely scanty,
It was her best, and she was vauntie.
Ah! little kent thy reverend grannie
That sark she coft for her wee Nannie
Wi' twa pund Scots ('twas a' her riches)
Was ever grac'd a dance of witches!
  But here my muse her wing maun cour;
Sic flights are far beyond her pow'r—

To sing how nannie lap and flang,
(A souple jade she was, and strang);
And how Tam stood, like ane bewitch'd,
And thought his very een enrich'd;
Even Satan glowr'd, and fidg'd fu' fain,
And hotch'd and blew wi' might and main:
Till first ae caper, syne anither,
Tam tint his reason a' thegither,
And roars out 'Weel done, Cutty-sark!'
And in an instant all was dark!
And scarcely had he Maggie rallied,
When out the hellish legion sallied.
  As bees bizz out wi' angry fyke
When plundering herds assail their byke,
As open pussie's mortal foes
When pop! she starts before their nose,
As eager runs the market-crowd,
When 'Catch the thief!' resounds aloud.
So Maggie runs; the witches follow,
Wi' mony an eldritch skriech and hollow.
  Ah, Tam! ah, Tam! thou'll get thy fairin'!
In hell they'll roast thee like a herrin'!
In vain thy Kate awaits thy comin'!
Kate soon will be a woefu' woman!
Now do thy speedy utmost, Meg,
And win the key-stane o' the brig:
There at them thou thy tail may toss,
A running stream they darena cross.
But ere the key-stane she could make,
The fient a tail she had to shake!

Douglas Byng (1893–   )

Millie the Mermaid

A Lament

If all the filth the seas provide
Was placed together side by side
With wreckage washed up by the tide
You'd get a sketch of me.

Down in the depths where monsters leap,
And giant crabs their vigil keep,
While Father Neptune tries to sleep,
I take my morning tea.
I once was famous, fresh and fair,
The siren with the coral hair
And every mariner's despair—
The man-trap of the sea.
Ah! Well, those days have passed,
    I've lost my lure at last.

I'm Millie, a messy old mermaid,
Out and about all the day,
Combing my hair — what little is there—
And just shouting my voice away.
If I am a bit thin and p'raps minus a fin,
It's a sin to suppose that I show it.
What a failure I've been in the last forty years,
Every sailor I've seen must have wool in his ears,
If a whaler harpooned me I'd give him three cheers,
    I'm well on the rocks and I know it.

Look at me! Sitting on a barnacle to keep from slipping off the rocks. Oh! well! I suppose one must like it or limpit. It's about time something *did* happen to me! The only excitement I've had in the last ten years was when I was run into by a swordfish! I was in half-pounds before you could say 'knife' — but I managed to save the middle cut — a nice kettle of fish I'd been in. I'm not as agile as I was years ago! I was known as the Brightest Bubble of the Baltic, now they call me the middle-aged mess of the Mediterranean! And as for all this oil pollution — there isn't a winkle or a cockle clean enough to play with! And those conger eels are far too slippery. You never know where they get to once you've lured them into your sea-bed. I did meet a diver once. I was lying on the ocean and he came up to me and said: 'I'm looking for an old wreck that's sunk very low.' I said, 'That's me!' But nothing happened. I couldn't unrivet him in time. Even the fish won't speak to me now. Only yesterday when I was floating down the Gulf-stream I was cut by a couple of smelts. Oh! I have to be careful. I was born on the Equator. You girls talk about 'love's fond embraces' — you want to try a night out with an octopus and see what happens, especially if he takes you into a whirlpool! I was never out of one until Father Neptune came up from the bottom of the sea with his Trident in his hand. No wonder Venus came up on a shell — if she hadn't she'd have been a bit out of the drawing by the time she got to the Uffizi. Ah! Well! Those were the days — the days of smugglers and pirates. We girls were smuggled here and smuggled there. You never knew what old cave you'd wake up in, and as for the pirates, they may have been bad bold men, but whenever you saw them hoist their jolly-roger you knew there was going to be a party.

I'm Millie, a messy old mermaid,
Hanging out here on the line,
Singing my song, I've been here so long,
I'm very near pickled with brine.
Oh, I know I've gone stale and my shape's like a whale,
And my tail has got bunions below it,
When my throat went so dry shouting out 'Ship ahoys'
To a boat sailing by I just cried 'Hallo boys!'
But the only reply was a very rude noise.
I'm well on the rocks and a know it.

George Canning (1770–1827)

Ipecacuanha

Coughing in a shady grove
    Sat my Juliana,
Lozenges I gave my love,
    Ipecacuanha—
Full twenty from the lozenge box
    The greedy nymph did pick;
Then, sighing sadly, said to me—
    My Damon, I am sick.

Henry Carey (1687?–1743)

Namby Pamby

*A Panegyric on the New Versification
Address'd to A— P— Esq.*

Naughty Paughty Jack-a-Dandy,
Stole a Piece of Sugar Candy
From the Grocer's Shoppy-Shop,
And away did hoppy-hop.

All ye poets of the age,
All ye witlings of the stage,
Learn your jingles to reform,
Crop your numbers to conform.
Let your little verses flow
Gently, sweetly, row by row;
Let the verse the subject fit,
Little subject, little wit.
Namby-Pamby is your guide,
Albion's joy, Hibernia's pride,
Namby-Pamby, pilly-piss,
Rhimy-pim'd on Missy Miss
Tartaretta Tartaree,
From the navel to the knee;
That her father's gracy-grace
Might give him a placey place.

He no longer writes of Mammy
Andromache and her lammy,
Hanging-panging at the breast
Of a matron most distress'd.
Now the venal poet sings
Baby clouts and baby things,
Baby dolls and baby houses,
Little misses, little spouses,
Little playthings, little toys,
Little girls and little boys.
As an actor does his part,
So the nurses get by heart
Namby-Pamby's little rhimes,
Little jingles, little chimes,
To repeat to missy-miss,
Piddling ponds of pissy-piss;
Cracking-packing like a lady,
Or bye-bying in the crady.
Namby-Pamby's doubly mild,
Once a man, and twice a child;
To his hanging sleeves restor'd,
Now he foots it like a lord;
Now he pumps his little wits,
Shitting writes, and writing shits,
All by little tiny bits.

And methinks I hear him say,
Boys and girls, come out to play!
Moon do's shine as bright as day.

    Now my Namby-Pamby's found
Sitting on the friar's ground,
Picking silver, picking gold;
Namby-Pamby's never old.
Bally-cally, they begin,
Namby-Pamby still keeps in.
Namby-Pamby is no clown.
London Bridge is broken down;
Now he courts the gay ladee,
Dancing o'er the Lady-Lee.
Now he sings of Lick-spit Lyar,
Burning in the brimstone fire;
Lyar, lyar! Lick-spit, Lick,
Turn about the candle stick!
Now he sings of Jacky Horner,
Sitting in the chimney corner,
Eating of a Christmas pye,
Putting in his thumb, O fie!
Putting in, O fie! this thumb,
Pulling out, O strange, a plum.
Now he plays at Stee-Straw-Stire,
Then he sticks them in the mire,
Now he acts the grenadier,
Calling for a pot of beer.
Where's his money? He's forgot;
Get him gone, a drunken sot.
Now a cock-horse does he ride,
And anon on timber stride.
See and Saw, and Sacch'ry Down,
London is a gallant town!
Now he gathers riches in,
Thicker, faster, pin by pin;
Pins apiece to see his show,
Boys and girls flock row by row;
From their clothes the pins they take,
Risk a whipping for his sake;
From their cloaths the pins they pull
To fill Namby's cushion full.

So much wit at such an age
Does a genius great presage;
Secondchildhood gone and past,
Should he prove a man at last,
What must second manhood be
In a child so bright as he.

Guard him, ye poetic pow'rs,
Watch his minutes, watch his hours;
Let your tuneful nine inspire him;
Let the poets, one and all,
To his genius victims fall.

Lewis Carroll (Charles Dodgson) (1832–98)
Letters

To Mary MacDonald — 5 Nov. 1864

Do not suppose that I didn't *write*, hundreds of times: the difficulty has been with the *directing*. I directed the letters so violently at first, that they went far beyond the mark — some of them were picked up at the other end of Russia. Last week I made a very near shot, and actually succeeded in putting 'Earls Terrace, Kensington,' only I over-did the number, and put 12,000, instead of 12. If you inquire for the letter at No. 12,000, I dare say they'll give it to you. After that, I fell into a feeble state of health, and directed the letters so gently that one of them only reached the other side of the room. It's lying by the side of the window now.

To Mary MacDonald — 14 Nov. 1864

Once upon a time there was a little girl, and she had a cross old Uncle — and this little girl had promised to copy out for him a sonnet Mr Rossetti had written about Shakespeare. Well, she didn't do it, you know; and the poor old Uncle's nose kept getting longer and longer, and his temper getting shorter and shorter, and post after post went by, and no sonnet came — I leave off here to explain how they sent letters in those days: there were no gates, so the gate-posts weren't obliged to stay in one place — consequence of which, they went wandering all over the country — consequence of which, if you wanted to send a letter anywhere, all you had to do was to fasten it to a gate-post that was going in the proper direction (only they sometimes changed their minds, which was awkward). This was called 'sending a letter by the post'. They did things very simply in those days: if you had a lot of money you just dug a hole under the hedge and popped it in: then you said you had 'put it in the bank', and you felt quite comfortable about it. And the way they travelled was — there were railings on the side of the road, and they used to get up, and walk along the top, as steadily as they could, till they tumbled off — which they mostly did very soon. This was called 'travelling by rail'. — Now to return to the wicked little girl. The end of her was, that a great black WOLF came, and — I don't like to go on, but nothing was found of her afterwards, except three small bones.

To Mary MacDonald — 22 Jan. 1866

I want to know what you *mean* by calling yourself 'naughty' for not having written sooner! Naughty, indeed! Stuff and nonsense! Do you think *I'd* call myself naughty, if I hadn't written to you, say for fifty years? Not a bit! I'd just begin as usual: 'My dear Mary, fifty years ago, you asked me what to do for your kitten, as it had a toothache, and I have just remembered to write about it. Perhaps the toothache has gone off by this time — if not, wash it carefully in hasty-pudding, and give it four pin-cusions boiled in sealing-wax, and just dip the end of its tail in hot coffee. This remedy has never been known to fail.' There! *That's* the proper way to write!

To Dolly Argles — 18 May 1869

I intend to divide my time between Pekin and Peru, week and week about — both are nice, interesting places, Pekin being full of foxes and Peru of lilies. The inhabitants of the former place live entirely on the tails of foxes (with butter, you know) and those of the latter place live by putting lilies in their hair.

To Gaylor Simpson — 27 Dec. 1873

I *never* dance, unless I am allowed to do it *In my own peculiar way*. There is no use trying to describe it: it has to be seen to be believed. The last house I tried it in, the floor broke through. But then it was a poor sort of floor — the beams were only six inches thick, hardly worth calling beams at all: stone arches are much more sensible, when any dancing, *of my peculiar kind*, is to be done. Did you ever see the rhinoceros, and the hippopotamus, at the Zoological Gardens, trying to dance a minuet together? It is a touching sight.

To Gertrude Chataway — 28 Oct. 1876

You will be sorry, and surprised, and puzzled, to hear what a queer illness I have had ever since you went. I sent for the doctor, and said: 'Give me some medicine, for I'm tired.' He said: 'Nonsense and stuff! You don't want medicine: go to bed!' I said: 'No; it isn't the sort of tiredness that wants bed. I'm tired in the *face*.' He looked a little grave, and said: 'Oh, it's your *nose* that's tired: a person often talks too much when he thinks he nose a great deal.' I said: 'No; it isn't the nose. Perhaps it's the *hair*.' Then he looked rather grave, and said: '*Now* I understand: You've been playing too many hairs on the pianoforte.' 'No, indeed I haven't,' I said, 'and it isn't exactly the *hair*; it's more about the nose and chin.' Then he looked a good deal graver, and said: 'Have you been walking on your chin lately?' I said: 'No.' 'Well!' he said, 'it puzzles me very much. Do you think that it's the lips?' 'Of course!' I said. 'That's exactly what it is!' Then he looked very grave indeed, and said, 'I think you must have been giving too many kisses.' 'Well,' I said, 'I did give *one* kiss to a baby child, a little friend of mine.' 'Think again,' he said: 'Are you sure it was only *one*?' I thought again, and said: 'Perhaps it was eleven times.' Then the doctor said: 'You must not give her *any* more till your lips are quite rested again.' 'But what am I to do?' I said. 'Because, you see, I owe her a hundred and eighty-two more.' Then he looked so grave that the tears ran down his cheeks, and he said: 'You may send them to her in a box.'

So I have packed them all very carefully. Tell me if they come safe, or if any are lost on the way.

To Marion Richards — 26 Oct 1881

Sometimes I get *that* confused, I hardly know which is me and which is the inkstand. The confusion in one's mind doesn't so much matter — but when it comes to putting bread and butter, and orange marmalade, into the *inkstand*; and then dipping pens into *oneself*, and filling *oneself* up with ink, you know, it's horrid!

From Through the Looking-Glass, 1872
Jabberwocky

. . . There was a book lying near Alice on the table, and while she sat watching the White King (for she was still a little anxious about him, and had the ink all ready to throw over him, in case he fainted again),

she turned over the leaves, to find some part that she could read, '—
for it's all in some language I don't know,' she said to herself.

It was like this.

> *ykcowrebbaJ*
> sevot yhtils eht dna ,gillirb sawT'
> :ebaw eht ni elbmig dna eryg diD
> ,sevogorob eht erew ysmim llA
> .ebargtuo shtar emom eht dnA

She puzzled over this for some time, but at last a bright thought
struck her. 'Why, it's a Looking-glass book, of course! And if I hold it
up to a glass, the words will all go the right way again.'

This was the poem that Alice read:

Jabberwocky

'Twas brillig, and the slithy toves
   Did gyre and gimble in the wabe:
All mimsy were the borogoves,
   And the mome raths outgrabe.

'Beware the Jabberwock, my son!
   The jaws that bite, the claws that catch!
Beware the Jubjub bird, and shun
   The frumious Bandersnatch!'

He took his vorpal sword in hand:
   Long time the manxome foe he sought—
So rested he by the Tumtum tree,
   And stood awhile in thought.

And, as in uffish thought he stood,
   The Jabberwock, with eyes of flame,
Came whiffling through the tulgey wood,
   And burbled as it came!

One, two! One, two! And through and through
   The vorpal blade went snicker-snack!
He left it dead, and with its head
   He went galumphing back.

'And hast thou slain the Jabberwock?
  Come to my arms, my beamish boy!
O frabjous day! Callooh! Callay!'
  He chortled in his joy.

'Twas brillig, and the slithy toves
  Did gyre and gimble in the wabe:
All mimsy were the borogoves,
  And the mome raths outgrabe.

Humpty Dumpty

'You seem very clever at explaining words, Sir,' said Alice. 'Would you kindly tell me the meaning of the poem called "Jabberwocky"?'

'Let's hear it,' said Humpty Dumpty. 'I can explain all the poems that were ever invented — and a good many that haven't been invented just yet.'

This sounded very hopeful, so Alice repeated the first verse:

' 'Twas brillig, and the slithy toves
  Did gyre and gimble in the wabe:
All mimsy were the borogoves,
  And the mome raths outgrabe.'

'That's enough to begin with,' Humpty Dumpty interrupted: 'there are plenty of hard words there. "*Brillig*" means four o'clock in the afternoon—the time when you being *broiling* things for dinner.'

'That'll do very well,' said Alice: 'and "*slithy*"?'

'Well, "*slithy*" means "lithe and slimy". "Lithe" is the same as "active". You see it's like a portmanteau— there are two meanings packed up into one word.'

'I see it now,' Alice remarked thoughtfully: 'and what are "*toves*"?'

'Well, "*toves*" are something like badgers — they're something like lizards — and they're something like corkscrews.'

'They must be very curious-looking creatures.'

'They are that,' said Humpty Dumpty; 'also they make their nests under sun-dials—also they live on cheese.'

'And what's to "*gyre*" and to "*gimble*?"'

'To "*gyre*" is to go round and round like a gyroscope. To "*gimble*" is to make holes like a gimlet.'

'And "*the wabe*" is the grass-plot round a sun-dial, I suppose?' said Alice, surprised at her own ingenuity.

'Of course it is. It's called "*wabe*" you know, because it goes a long way before it, and a long way behind it—'

'And a long way beyond it on each side,' Alice added.

'Exactly so. Well then, "*mimsy*" is "flimsy and miserable" (there's another portmanteau for you). And a "*borogove*" is a thin shabby-looking bird with its feathers sticking out all round—something like a live mop.'

'And then "*mome raths*"?' said Alice. 'I'm afraid I'm giving you a great deal of trouble.'

'Well, a "*rath*" is a sort of green pig: but "*mome*" I'm not certain about. I think it's short for "from home"—meaning that they'd lost their way, you know.'

'And what does "*outgrabe*" mean?'

'Well, "*outgrabing*" is something between bellowing and whistling, with a kind of sneeze in the middle: however, you'll hear it done, maybe—down in the wood yonder—and, when you've once heard it, you'll be *quite* content. Who's been repeating all that hard stuff to you?'

'I read it in a book,' said Alice. 'But I *had* some poetry repeated to me much easier than that, by—Tweedledee, I think it was.'

'As to poetry, you know,' said Humpty Dumpty, stretching out one of his great hands, '*I* can repeat poetry as well as other folk, if it comes to that—'

'Oh, it needn't come to that!' Alice hastily said, hoping to keep him from beginning.

Looking Glass Insects

'Tickets, please!' said the Guard, putting his head in at the window. In a moment everybody was holding out a ticket: they were about the same size as the people, and quite seemed to fill the carriage.

'Now then! Show your ticket, child!' the Guard went on, looking angrily at Alice. And a great many voices all said together ('like the chorus of a song,' thought Alice) 'Don't keep him waiting, child! Why, his time is worth a thousand pounds a minute!'

'I'm afraid I haven't got one,' Alice said in a frightened tone: 'there wasn't a ticket-office where I came from.' And again the chorus of voices went on. 'There wasn't room for one where she came from. The land there is worth a thousand pounds an inch!'

'Don't make excuses,' said the Guard: 'You should have bought one from the engine-driver.' And once more the chorus of voices went on with 'The man that drives the engine. Why, the smoke alone is worth a thousand pounds a puff!'

Alice thought to herself 'Then there's no use in speaking.' The voices didn't join in, *this* time, as she hadn't spoken, but, to her great surprise, they all *thought* in chorus (I hope you understand what *thinking in chorus* means — for I must confess that *I* don't). 'Better say nothing at all. Language is worth a thousand pounds a word!'

'I shall dream about a thousand pounds tonight, I know I shall!' thought Alice.

All this time the Guard was looking at her, first through a telescope, then through a microscope, and then through an opera-glass. At last he said 'You're travelling the wrong way,' and shut up the window, and went away.

'So young a child,' said the gentleman sitting opposite to her, (he was dressed in white paper), 'ought to know which way she's going, even if she doesn't know her own name!'

A Goat that was sitting next to the gentleman in white, shut his

eyes and said in a loud voice, 'She ought to know her way to the
ticket-office, even if she doesn't know her alphabet!'

There was a Beetle sitting next to the Goat (it was a very queer
carriage-full of passengers altogether), and, as the rule seemed to be
that they should all speak in turn, *he* went on with 'She'll have to go
back from here as luggage!'

Alice couldn't see who was sitting beyond the Beetle, but a hoarse
voice spoke next. 'Change engines—' it said, and there it choked and
was obliged to leave off.

The Walrus and the Carpenter

The sun was shining on the sea,
　Shining with all his might:
He did his very best to make
　The billows smooth and bright—
And this was odd, because it was
　The middle of the night.

The moon was shining sulkily,
   Because she thought the sun
Had got no business to be there
   After the day was done—
'It's very rude of him,' she said,
   'To come and spoil the fun!'

The sea was wet as wet could be,
   The sands were dry as dry.
You could not see a cloud, because
   No cloud was in the sky:
No birds were flying overhead—
   There were no birds to fly.

The Walrus and the Carpenter
   Were walking close at hand:
They wept like anything to see
   Such quantities of sand:
'If this were only cleared away,'
   They said, 'it *would* be grand!'

'If seven maids with seven mops
  Swept if for half a year,
Do you suppose,' the Walrus said,
  'That they could get it clear?'
'I doubt it,' said the Carpenter,
  And shed a bitter tear.

'O Oysters, come and walk with us!'
  The Walrus did beseech.
'A pleasant walk, a pleasant talk,
  Along the briny beach;
We cannot do with more than four,
  To give a hand to each.'

The eldest Oyster looked at him,
  But never a word he said:
The eldest Oyster winked his eye,
  And shook his heavy head—
Meaning to say he did not choose
  To leave the oyster-bed.

But four young Oysters hurried up,
  All eager for the treat:
Their coats were brushed, their faces washed,
  Their shoes were clean and neat—
And this was odd, because, you know,
  They hadn't any feet.

Four other Oysters followed them,
  And yet another four;
And thick and fast they came at last,
  And more, and more, and more—
All hopping through the frothy waves,
  And scrambling to the shore.

The Walrus and the Carpenter
  Walked on a mile or so,
And then they rested on a rock
  Conveniently low:
And all the little Oysters stood
  And waited in a row.

'The time has come,' the Walrus said,
   'To talk of many things:
Of shoes — and ships — and sealing wax—
   Of cabbages — and kings—
And why the sea is boiling hot—
   And whether pigs have wings.'

'But wait a bit,' the Oysters cried,
   'Before we have our chat:
For some of us are out of breath,
   And all of us are fat!'
'No hurry!' said the Carpenter.
   They thanked him much for that.

'A loaf of bread,' the Walrus said,
   'Is what we chiefly need:
Pepper and vinegar besides
   Are very good indeed—
Now, if you're ready, Oysters dear,
   We can begin to feed.'

'But not on us!' the Oysters cried,
    Turning a little blue.
'After such kindness, that would be
    A dismal thing to do!'
'The night is fine,' the Walrus said.
    'Do you admire the view?

'It was so kind of you to come!
    And you are very nice!'
The Carpenter said nothing but
    'Cut us another slice.
I wish you were not quite so deaf—
    I've had to ask you twice!'

'It seems a shame,' the Walrus said,
    'To play them such a trick.
After we've brought them out so far,
    And made them trot so quick!'
The Carpenter said nothing but
    'The butter's spread too thick!'

'I weep for you,' the Walrus said:
　'I deeply sympathise.'
With sobs and tears he sorted out
　Those of the largest size,
Holding his pocket-hankerchief
　Before his streaming eyes.

'O Oysters,' said the Carpenter,
　'You've had a pleasant run!
Shall we be trotting home again?'
　But answer came there none—
And this was scarcely odd, because
　They'd eaten every one.

From Sylvie and Bruno — 1889

'You must explain to me, please,' the Professor said with an anxious look, '*which* is the Lion, and *which* is the Gardener. It's *most* important not to get two such animals confused together. And one's very likely to do it in their case — both having mouths, you know.

'Now, for instance, there's the rabbit hutch and the hall clock. One gets a little confused with *them* — both having doors, you know. Now, only yesterday — would you believe it? — I put some lettuces into the clock, and tried to wind up the rabbit!'

'Did the rabbit *go*, after you wound it up?' said Bruno.

'Go? I should think it *did* go! And wherever it's gone to — that's what I can't find out!'

From Sylvie and Bruno, Concluded — 1893

'Our Second Experiment,' the Professor announced, 'is the production of Black Light! You have seen White Light, Red Light, Green Light, and so on: but never, till this wonderful day, have any eyes but mine seen *Black Light!* This box,' carefully lifting it upon the table, and covering it with a heap of blankets, 'is quite full of it. The way I made it was this — I took a lighted candle into a dark cupboard and shut the door. Of course the cupboard was then full of *Yellow* Light. Then I took a bottle of Black ink, and poured it over the candle: and, to my delight, every atom of the Yellow Light turned *BLACK!* Then I filled a box with it. And now — would anyone like to get under the blankets and see it?'

Bruno crawled under the blankets, and after a minute or two crawled out again.

'What did you see in the box?' Sylvie eagerly inquired.

'I saw *nothing!*' Bruno sadly replied. 'It were too dark!'

'He has described the appearance of the thing exactly!' the Professor exclaimed with enthusiasm. 'Black Light, and Nothing, look so extremely alike, at first sight, that I don't wonder he failed to distinguish them!'

G. K. Chesterton (1874–1936)

Wine and Water

Old Noah he had an ostrich farm and fowls on the
    largest scale,
He ate his egg with a ladle in an egg-cup big as a pail,
And the soup he took was Elephant Soup and the fish he
    took was Whale,
But they all were small to the cellar he took when he set
    out to sail,
And Noah he often said to his wife when he sat down
    to dine,
'I don't care where the water goes if it doesn't get into
    the wine.'

The cataract of the cliff of heaven fell blinding off
    the brink
As if it would wash the stars away as suds go down a
    sink,
The seven heavens came roaring down for the throats of
    hell to drink,
And Noah he cocked his eye and said, 'It looks like rain,
    I think,
The water has drowned the Matterhorn as deep as a
    Mendip mine,
But I don't care where the water goes if it doesn't get
    into the wine.'

But Noah he sinned, and we have sinned; on tipsy feet
    we trod,

Till a great big black teetotaller was sent to us for a
     rod,
And you can't get wine at a P.S.A., or chapel, or
     Eisteddfod,
For the Curse of Water has come again because of the
     wrath of God,
And water is on the Bishop's board and the Higher
     Thinker's shrine,
But I don't care where the water goes if it doesn't
     get into the wine.

Samuel Taylor Coleridge (1772–1834)
The House That Jack Built

And this reft house is that the which he built,
Lamented Jack! and here his malt he piled.
Cautious in vain! these rats that squeak so wild,
Squeak not unconscious of their father's guilt.
Did he not see her gleaming through the glade?
Belike 'twas she, the maiden all forlorn.
What though she milked no cow with crumpled horn,
Yet, *aye* she haunts the dale where *erst* she strayed:
And *aye* before her stalks her amorous knight!
Still on his thighs their wonted brogues are worn,
And through those brogues, still tattered and betorn,
His hindward charms gleam an unearthly white;
As when through broken clouds at night's high noon
Peeps in fair fragments forth the full-orbed harvest-moon.

Frank Davies (1911–   )
Song in Outer Esquimo Dialect

Quingwam quingwam
frillybim frillybim
floop floop floop floop
prim fripple frapple bimstock
oorst voorst pimchik blik
mimsey mimsey chittle fim
chillibimsnooknok

irrysparry plingdong
irrysparry plingdong
tootootootootootootootootoot!

Rough translation:
    Now that Mamook has eaten the duck
    We must send out the hunters.
    Is there never an end to blubber?
    Why are the reindeers coughing?

All Our Yesterdays

Apes and men had a common ancestor
who roamed for a while and settled near Manchester;
this is no reflection on Mancunians,
we're all the results of rather hideous unions.

John Davies of Hereford (1565?–1618)

'The Author Loving these Homely Meats Specially, viz: Cream,
Pancakes, Buttered Pippin-pies (Laugh, Good People) and
Tobacco; Writ to that Worthy and Virtuous Gentlewoman,
whom He Calleth Mistress, as Followeth'

If there were, oh! an Hellespont of cream
Between us, milk-white mistress, I would swim
To you, to show to both my love's extreme,
Leander-like, — yea! dive from brim to brim.
But met I with a buttered pippin-pie
Floating upon 't, that would I make my boat
To waft me to you without jeopardy,
Though sea-sick I might be while it did float.
Yet if a storm should rise, by night or day,
Of sugar-snows and hail of caraways,
Then, if I found a pancake in my way,
It like a plank should bring me to your kays;
    Which having found, if they tobacco kept,
    The smoke should dry me well before I slept.

Charles Dickens (1812–70)

From Pickwick Papers

Mr Weller having obtained leave of absence from Mr Pickwick, who, in his then state of excitement and worry, was by no means displeased at being left alone, set forth, long before the appointed hour, and having plenty of time at his disposal, sauntered down as far as the Mansion House, where he paused and contemplated, with a face of great calmness and philosophy, the numerous cads and drivers of short stages who assemble near that famous place of resort, to the great terror and confusion of the old-lady population of these realms. Having loitered here, for half an hour or so, Mr Weller turned, and began wending his way towards Leadenhall Market, through a variety of by-streets and courts. As he was sauntering away his spare time, and stopped to look at almost every object that met his gaze, it is by no means surprising that Mr Weller should have paused before a small stationer's and print-seller's window; but without further explanation it does appear surprising that his eyes should have no sooner rested on certain pictures which were exposed for sale therein, than he gave a sudden start, smote his right leg with great vehemence, and exclaimed, with energy, 'If it hadn't been for this, I should ha' forgot all about it, till it was too late!'

The particular picture on which Sam Weller's eyes were fixed, as he said this, was a highly-coloured representation of a couple of human hearts skewered together with an arrow, cooking before a cheerful fire, while a male and female cannibal in modern attire, the gentleman being clad in a blue coat and white trousers, and the lady in a deep red pelisse with a parasol of the same, were approaching the meal with hungry eyes, up a serpentine gravel path leading thereunto. A decidedly indelicate young gentleman, in a pair of wings and nothing else, was depicted as superintending the cooking; a representation of the spire of the church in Langham Place, London, appeared in the distance; and the whole formed a 'valentine', of which, as a written inscription in the window testified, there was a large assortment within, which the shopkeeper pledged himself to dispose of, to his countrymen generally, at the reduced rate of one-and-sixpence each.

'I should ha' forgot it; I should certainly ha' forgot it!' said Sam; so saying, he at once stepped into the stationer's shop, and requested to be served with a sheet of the best gilt-edged letter-paper, and a hard-nibbed pen which could be warranted not to splutter. These articles having been promptly supplied, he walked on direct towards

Leadenhall Market at a good round pace, very different from his recent lingering one. Looking round him, he there beheld a signboard on which the painter's art had delineated something remotely resembling a cerulean elephant with an aquiline nose in lieu of trunk. Rightly conjecturing that this was the Blue Boar himself, he stepped into the house, and inquired concerning his parent.

'He won't be here this three-quarters of an hour or more,' said the young lady who superintended the domestic arrangements of the Blue Boar.

'Wery good, my dear,' replied Sam. 'Let me have nine-penn'oth o' brandy-and-water luke, and the inkstand, will you, miss?'

The brandy-and-water luke, and the inkstand, having been carried into the little parlour, and the young lady having carefully flattened down the coals to prevent their blazing, and carried away the poker to preclude the possibility of the fire being stirred, without the full privity and concurrence of the Blue Boar being first had and obtained, Sam Weller sat himself down in a box near the stove, and pulled out the sheet of gilt-edged letter-paper, and the hard-nibbed pen. Then looking carefully at the pen to see that there were no hairs in it, and dusting down the table, so that there might be no crumbs of bread under the paper, Sam tucked up the cuffs of his coat, and squared his elbows, and composed himself to write.

To ladies and gentlemen who are not in the habit of devoting themselves practically to the science of penmanship, writing a letter is no very easy task; it being always considered necessary in such cases for the writer to recline his head on his left arm, so as to place his eyes as nearly as possible on a level with the paper, and, while glancing sideways at the letters he is constructing, to form with his tongue imaginary characters to correspond. These motions, although unquestionably of the greatest assistance to original composition, retard in some degree the progress of the writer; and Sam had unconsciously been a full hour and a half writing words in small text, smearing out wrong letters with his little finger, and putting in new ones which required going over very often to render them visible through the old blots, when he was roused by the opening of the door and the entrance of his parent.

'Vell, Sammy,' said the father.

'Vell, my Prooshan Blue,' responded the son, laying down his pen. 'What's the last bulletin about mother-in-law?'

'Mrs Veller passed a very good night, but is uncommon perwerse, and unpleasant this mornin'. Signed upon oath, Tony Veller, Esquire. That's the last vun as was issued, Sammy,' replied Mr Weller, untying his shawl.

'No better yet?' inquired Sam.

'All the symptoms aggerawated,' replied Mr Weller, shaking his head. 'But wot's that, you're a-doin' of? Pursuit of knowledge under difficulties, Sammy?'

'I've done now,' said Sam, with slight embarrassment; 'I've been a-writin'.'

'So I see,' replied Mr Weller. 'Not to any young 'ooman, I hope, Sammy?'

'Why, it's no use a-sayin' it ain't,' replied Sam; 'it's a walentine.'

'A what!' exclaimed Mr Weller, apparently horror-stricken by the word.

'A walentine,' replied Sam.

'Samivel, Samivel,' said Mr Weller, in reproachful accents, 'I didn't think you'd ha' done it. Arter the warnin' you've had o' your father's wicious propensities; arter all I've said to you upon this here wery subject; arter actiwally seein' and bein' in the company o' your own mother-in-law, vich I should ha' thought wos a moral-lesson as no man could never ha' forgotton to his dyin' day! I didn't think you'd ha' done it, Sammy, I didn't think you'd ha' done it!' These reflections were too much for the good old man. He raised Sam's tumbler to his lips and drank off its contents.

'Wot's the matter now?' said Sam.

'Nev'r mind, Sammy,' replied Mr Weller, 'it'll be a wery agonisin' trial to me at my time of life, but I'm pretty tough, that's vun consolation, as the wery old turkey remarked wen the farmer said he wos afeerd he should be obliged to kill him for the London market.'

'Wot'll be a trial?' inquired Sam.

'To see you married, Sammy — to see you a dilluded wictim, and thinkin' in your innocence that it's all wery capital,' replied Mr Weller. 'It's a dreadful trial to a father's feelin's, that 'ere, Sammy.'

'Nonsense,' said Sam. 'I ain't a-goin' to get married, don't you fret yourself about that; I know you're a judge of these things. Order in your pipe and I'll read you the letter. There!'

We cannot distinctly say whether it was the prospect of the pipe, or the consolatory reflection that a fatal disposition to get married ran in the family, and couldn't be helped, which calmed Mr Weller's feelings, and caused his grief to subside. We should be rather disposed to say that the result was attained by combining the two sources of consolation, for he repeated the second in a low tone, very frequently; ringing the bell meanwhile, to order in the first. He then divested himself of his upper coat; and lighting the pipe and placing himself in front of the fire with his back towards it, so that he could feel its full heat, and recline against the mantel-piece at the same time, turned towards Sam, and, with a countenance greatly mollified by the softening influence of tobacco, requested him to 'fire away.'

Sam dipped his pen into the ink to be ready for any corrections, and began with a very theatrical air —

'"Lovely—"'

'Stop,' said Mr Weller, ringing the bell. 'A double glass o' the inwariable, my dear.'

'Very well, sir,' replied the girl; who with great quickness appeared, vanished, returned, and disappeared.

'They seem to know your ways here,' observed Sam.

'Yes,' replied his father, 'I've been here before in my time. Go on, Sammy.'

'"Lovely creetur,"' repeated Sam.

''Tain't in poetry, is it?' interposed his father.

'No, no,' replied Sam.

'Wery glad to hear it,' said Mr Weller. 'Poetry's unnat'ral; no man ever talked poetry 'cept a beadle on boxing-day, or Warren's blackin, or Rowland's oil, or some of them low fellows; never you let yourself down to talk poetry, my boy. Begin again, Sammy.'

Mr Weller resumed his pipe with critical solemnity, and Sam once more commenced, and read as follows:-

'"Lovely creetur I feel myself a damned—",'

'That ain't proper,' said Mr Weller, taking his pipe from his mouth.

'No; it ain't "damned,"' observed Sam, holding the letter up to the light, 'it's "shamed," there's a blot there — "I feel myself ashamed."'

'Wery good,' said Mr Weller. 'Go on.'

'"Feel myself ashamed, and completely cir—" I forget what this here word is,' said Sam, scratching his head with the pen, in vain attempts to remember.

'Why don't you look at it, then?' inquired Mr Weller.

'So I am a-lookin' at it,' replied Sam, but there's another blot. Here's a "c," and a "i," and a "d."'

'Circumwented, p'raps,' suggested Mr Weller.

'No, it ain't that,' said Sam, '"circumscribed"; that's it.'

'That ain't as good a word as "circumwented," Sammy,' said Mr Weller gravely.

'Think not?' said Sam.

'Nothin' like it,' replied his father.

'But don't you think it means more?' inquired Sam.

'Vell, p'raps it's a more tenderer word,' said Mr Weller, after a few moments' reflection. 'Go on, Sammy.'

'"Feel myself ashamed and completely circumscribed in a-dressin' of you, for you *are* a nice gal and nothin' but it."'

'That's a wery pretty sentiment,' said the elder Mr Weller, removing his pipe to make way for the remark.

'Yes, I think it is rayther good,' observed Sam, highly flattered.

'Wot I like in that 'ere style of writin',' said the elder Mr Weller, 'is, that their ain't no callin' names in it — no Wenuses, nor nothin' o' that kind. Wot's the good o' callin' a young 'ooman a Wenus or a angel, Sammy?'

'Ah! what, indeed?' replied Sam.

'You might just as well call her a griffin, or a unicorn, or a king's arms at once, which is wery well known to be a collection o' fabulous animals,' added Mr Weller.

'Just as well,' replied Sam.

'Drive on, Sammy,' said Mr Weller.

Sam complied with the request, and proceeded as follows; his father continuing to smoke, with a mixed expression of wisdom and complacency, which was particularly edifying.'

'"Afore I see you, I thought all women was alike."'

'So they are,' observed the elder Mr Weller parenthetically.

'"But now," continued Sam, "now I find what a reg'lar soft-headed, inkred'lous turnip I must ha' been; for there ain't nobody like you, though I like you better than nothin' at all." I thought it best to make that rayther strong,' said Sam, looking up.

Mr Weller nodded approvingly, and Sam resumed.

'"So I take the privilidge of the day, Mary, my dear – as the gen'l'm'n in difficulties did, ven he valked out of a Sunday — to tell you that the first and only time I see you, your likeness was took on my hart in much quicker time and brighter colours than ever a likeness was took by the profeel macheen (wich p'raps you may have heerd on Mary my dear) altho it *does* finish a portrait and put the frame and glass on complete, with a hook at the end to hang it up by, and all in two minutes and a quarter."'

'I am afeered that werges on the poetical, Sammy,' said Mr Weller dubiously.

'No, it don't,' replied Sam, reading on very quickly, to avoid contesting the point—

'"Except of me Mary my dear as your walentine and think over what I've said. — My dear Mary I will now conclude." That's all,' said Sam.

'That's rather a sudden pull-up, ain't it, Sammy?' inquired Mr Weller.

'Not a bit on it,' said Sam; 'she'll vish there wos more, and that's the great art o' letter-writin'.'

'Well,' said Mr Weller, 'there's somethin' in that; and I wish your mother-in-law 'ud only conduct her conwersation on the same genteel principle. Ain't you a-goin' to sign it?'

'That's the difficulty,' said Sam; 'I don't know what to sign it.'

'Sign it — "Veller"', said the oldest surviving proprietor of that name.

'Won't do,' said Sam. 'Never sign a walentine with your own name.'

'Sign it "Pickwick." then,' said Mr Weller; 'it's a wery good name, and a easy one to spell.'

'The wery thing,' said Sam. 'I could end with a werse; what do you think?'

'I don't like it, Sam,' rejoined Mr Weller. 'I never know'd a respectable coachman as wrote poetry, 'cept one, as made an affectin' copy o' werses the night afore he was hung for a highway robbery; and he wos only a Cambervell man, so even that's no rule.'

But Sam was not to be dissuaded from the poetical idea that had occurred to him, so he signed the letter—

'Your love-sick
Pickwick.'

From Nicholas Nickleby

'This is the first class in English spelling and philosophy, Nickleby,' said Squeers, beckoning Nicholas to stand beside him. 'We'll get up a Latin one, and hand that over to you. Now, then, where's the first boy?'

'Please, sir, he's cleaning the back parlour window,' said the temporary head of the philosophical class.

'So he is, to be sure,' rejoined Squeers. 'We go upon the practical mode of teaching, Nickleby; the regular education system. C-l-e-a-n, clean, verb active, to make bright, to scour. W-i-n, win, d-e-r, winder, a casement. When the boy knows this out of the book, he goes and does it. It's just the same principle as the use of the globes. Where's the second boy?'

'Please, sir, he's weeding the garden,' replied a small voice.

'To be sure,' said Squeers, by no means disconcerted. 'So he is. B-o-t, bot, t-i-n. n-e-y, bottiney, noun substantive, a knowledge of plants. When he has learned that bottinney means a knowledge of plants, he goes and knows 'em. That's our system, Nickleby; what do you think of it?'

'It's a very useful one, at any rate,' answered Nicholas.

'I believe you,' rejoined Squeers, not remarking the emphasis of his usher. 'Third boy, what's a horse?'

'A beast, sir,' replied the boy.

'So it is,' said Squeers. 'Ain't it, Nickleby?'

'I believe there is no doubt of that, sir,' answered Nicholas.

'Of course there isn't,' said Squeers. 'A horse is a quadruped, and quadruped's Latin for beast, as everybody that's gone through the grammar knows, or else where's the use of having grammars at all?'

'Where, indeed!' said Nicholas abstractedly.

'As you're perfect in that,' resumed Squeers, turning to the boy, 'go and look after *my* horse, and rub him down well, or I'll rub you down. The rest of the class go and draw water up, till somebody tells you to leave off, for it's washing-day tomorrow, and they want the coppers filled.'

W. C. Fields (1879–1946)

From Never Give a Sucker an Even Break

Original story: Otis Criblecoblis (W. C. Fields)

Screenplay: John T. Neville, Prescott Chaplin

(. . . *The rear platform of the giant airliner is open to the clouds, as on the back of an old continental train. FIELDS comes over, and we pan with him as he sits. He takes a glass of water from the table and throws it overboard. The slipstream of the airliner throws it right back in his face.*)

W. C. FIELDS:	What inclement weather!
	(*He takes a whisky bottle from his pocket and pours himself a drink, then he stands the bottle on the window-ledge of the platform. GLORIA comes up behind him*)
GLORIA:	What are you drinking, Uncle Bill?
W. C. FIELDS:	Oh, just a little ginger ale, dear. Pull up a chair.
	(*GLORIA pulls up a chair and sits beside her uncle*)
GLORIA:	(*earnestly*): You know, Uncle Bill, I've been thinking. Why didn't you ever marry?

W. C. FIELDS: I was in love with a beautiful blonde once, dear. She drove me to drink. That's the one thing I'm indebted to her for.

(FIELDS now wants another drink, so he is full of good advice)

W. C. FIELDS: Go in and push your little portmanteau, will you dear?

GLORIA: All right.

(Track back as she rises and leaves the rear platform. As she goes, FIELDS starts to reach for his whisky bottle. He is not looking properly and knocks the bottle off the window ledge. He rises, appalled. Quickly he dives over the edge of the aeroplane. GLORIA runs back to the window)

GLORIA: Uncle Bill!

(Another trick shot shows FIELDS still falling through the clouds. He catches up with the whisky bottle, grabs it, pulls the cork out of the air, and caps the bottle. From high above, we see a large house surrounded by gardens in the mountains.

Now we are in the gardens, as the beautiful young OULIOTTA HEMOGLOBEN goes over to the divan and lies upon it. Close now on OULIOTTA, as we see her looking up from the pillows and rising in surprise, as a human bomb hurtles down. Another trick shot shows FIELDS still falling through the clouds, as he poises his hands, ready to dive.

OULIOTTA runs from the divan and crosses the terrace to the steps. Shot from directly overhead we see FIELDS falling onto the divan with the sound of thunder, then bouncing up again, while OULIOTTA watches him from the terrace.

OULIOTTA is bewildered, but beautifully so. FIELDS is still bouncing up and down on the divan. Finally, he reaches equipoise, or somewhat near.

OULIOTTA goes on watching him, unable to believe her eyes. FIELDS slowly gets to his feet, as OULIOTTA comes on. He doesn't notice her at first, then does a double take when he does)

W. C. FIELDS: Ah, why didn't I think of that parachute? Well, there she goes! What a bump! And how unfortunate . . . ah, ah, how do you do?

(He approaches the amazed OULIOTTA)

W. C. FIELDS: Uh . . . you live here?
OULIOTTA: What are you?
W. C. FIELDS: I am an American citizen.
OULIOTTA: An American eagle?
W. C. FIELDS: Why, no, first time I have ever been up in a plane in my life. I'm. . . . uh . . . just a man.
OULIOTTA: Man? I have never heard that word before.
W. C. FIELDS: You didn't?
OULIOTTA: Are you really a man?
W. C. FIELDS: Well, I have been called other things.

(Perplexed, the lovely OULIOTTA eyes her first man)

OULIOTTA: I have never seen one before in all my life.

(FIELDS relishes the dialogue, seeing nobody else near)

W. C. FIELDS: You never have . . . eh?
OULIOTTA: Mother brought me to the nest here when I was only three months old.
W. C. FIELDS: Oh, she did, eh? You have never seen a man? Have you ever played the game of Squidgilum?

(OULIOTTA shakes her head in sorrow)

OULIOTTA: No, the only game I have ever played is bean bag.

(FIELDS sees his chance, and gets a chair)

W. C. FIELDS: Bean bag? Hm . . . that's very good. It becomes very exciting at times. I saw the championship played in Paris. Many people were killed. Pull up a chair.

(Obediently OULIOTTA pulls up a chair close to his chair and sits down)

W. C. FIELDS: Get a little closer. Wait a minute, maybe I'm the one.

(He puts his hands over his head as he starts to explain the game)

W. C. FIELDS: Uh, now you put your hands on your head that way.

(Now she puts her hands over her head and follows his game plan)

W. C. FIELDS: That's it. Now close your eyes and pucker your lips a bit.

(He leans over and kisses her.
OULIOTTA is now seen in a large close-up. FIELDS, with his back to us, withdraws. She opens her eyes and lowers her arms, then decides that she likes the game.
So she puts her arms over her head again, closes her eyes and puckers up her mouth.
FIELDS does another double take to see OULIOTTA ready, willing and able again. So he gives her a second kiss. Then she lowers her arms.
From the house, OULIOTTA's black-clad ogre of a mother.
MRS HEMOGLOBEN appears, holding a Great Dane with vampire fangs on a leash.
The Great Dane looks gigantic, seen in close-up and movement.
Now the Great Lover is seen in close-up and delighted)

W. C. FIELDS: Ah . . . shall we play another rubber?

(OULIOTTA smiles, then hears the Great Dane growl, and she looks off)

OULIOTTA: Why, Mother!

(FIELDS now looks around, scared at the canine and maternal menace.
The Great Dane's head slavers at him.
MRS HEMOGLOBEN's face glares at him.
FIELDS decides to brave it out beside OULIOTTA)

W. C. FIELDS: Romulus and Remus!

Samuel Foote (1720–77)

The Grand Panjamdrum

So she went into the garden to cut a cabbage leaf, to make an apple pie; and at the same time a great she-bear coming up the street, pops its head into the shop. 'What! no soap?' So he died, and she very imprudently married the barber; and there were present the Picninnies, and the Joblillies, and the Garyulies, and the grand Panjamdrum himself, with the little round button at top; and they all fell to playing the game of catch as catch can, till the gunpowder ran out at the heels of their boots.

W. S. Gilbert (1836–1911)

The Student

From The Bab Ballads

I have chambers up in Gray's-inn,
 Turning out from Holborn-bars,
Though there are as many ways in
 As in Dublin there are cars.

You from Gray's-inn-lane can enter,
 or from *.* among the trees,
Then there's * * in the centre,
 Or from * *, if you please.

(Here follows, in thirteen verses, a list of the various approaches to Gray's-inn.)

I am on the second story,
 Where my name, in sable tint,
You may find in all the glory
 Of the largest Roman print.

If you'd like to know what others
 Live within the same domain,
Why there's, first, COLLUMPTON BROTHERS,
 Then there's POGSON, COGS, and CRANE.

Then you come to—

(Here follow, in seven verses, the names of our contributor's fellow-lodgers.)

One fine morning I was sitting
    On my pleasant window-sill,
Little o'er my mind was flitting,
    As I nibbled at my quill,

Not of Mexico revolving,
    Nor of Portugal and Spain,
Nor of Parliament dissolving,
    Nor of smashed excursion train.

(Here, in twenty-seven verses, follows a list of subjects of which our contributor was not thinking.)

For of Mexico I'm weary,
    Parliament's a thing of nought,
Trains to me are always dreary—
    Trains of passengers or thought.

(Here, in nineteen verses, he explains his reasons for not thinking of the subjects enumerated in the preceding twenty-seven.)

Well, as I was sitting idly
    On my pleasant window-sill,
Speculating vaguely, widely,
    On my aunt's unopened will,

I perceived a silent student
    At a window, quite at home,
Stooping more than I thought prudent
    Over a Tremendous Tome.

As I watched the youth pursuing
    His * * * I exclaimed,
'Well I wonder what you're doing,
    And I wonder how you're named!'

P'raps to orders you're proceeding,
   P'raps I've found a lawyer keen—
Caught an Oxford man at Reading—
   Possibly your name is GREEN.

(Here, in thirty-five verses, he speculates on the youth's possible prospects, and suggests a variety of names, all or any of which may be his. He then, rather artistically, changes his metre, and bursts into the following impassioned appeal):-

   'I ask an ap-
     It is zo-
     Is it conch-
     Is it ge-
     'Lectro bi-
     Meteor-
     Is it nos-   ology?'
     Or ctym-
     P'raps it's myth-
     Is it the-
     Palaeont-
     Or archae-

(And so on, through all the ologies — eighty-four more lines.)

This in accents loud I shouted
   At the youth across the square,
* * * I never doubted
   * * * he was aware.

   'I ask an ap-
     It is zo-
     Is it conch-   ology?'
     Is it ge-

(And so on, as before, through the ninety-six ologies.)

Still no answer, sign, or motion
   Came from him across to me,
And to this day I've no notion
   What the student's lore might be,

Whether zo-
Whether conch-　　　ology,
Whether ge-

(And so on, as above.)

A. D. Godley (1856–1925)

On the Motor Bus

What is this that roareth thus?
Can it be a Motor Bus?
Yes, the smell and hideous hum
Indicat Motorem Bum!
Implet in the Corn and High
Terror me Motoris Bi:
Bo Motori clamitabo
Ne Motore caedar a Bo—
Dative be or Ablative
So thou only let us live:-
Whither shall thy victims flee?
Spare us, spare us, Motor Be!
Thus I sang; and still anigh
Came in hordes Motores Bi,
Et complebat omne forum
Copia Motorum Borum.
How shall wretches live like us
Cincti Bis Motoribus?
Domine, defende nos
Contra hos Motores Bos!

In Memoriam Examinatoris Cuiusdam

Lo, where you undistinguished grave
　　Erects its grassy pile on
One who to all Experience gave
　　An Alpha or Epsilon.

The world and eke the world's content,
　　And all therein that passes, .
With marks numerical (per cent)
　　He did dispose in classes:

Not his to ape the critic crew
　　Which vulgarly appraises
The Good, the Beautiful, the True
　　In literary phrases:

He did his estimate express
　　In terms precise and weighty,–
And Vice for 25 (or less),
　　While Virtue rose to 80.

Now hath he closed his earthly lot
　　All in his final heaven, –
(And be the stone that marks the spot
　　On one side only graven);[1]

Bring papers on his grave to strew
　　Amid the grass and clover,
And plant thereby that pencil blue
　　Wherewith he looked them over!

There freed from every human ill
　　And fleshly trammels gross, he
Lies in his resting place until
　　The final Viva Voce:

So let him rest till crack of doom,
　　Of mortal tasks aweary, –
And nothing write upon his tomb
　　Save β– (?).

[1]Candidates in University examinations are requested to write 'on one side of their paper only'.

Oliver Goldsmith (1728–74)

Elegy on the Death of a Mad Dog

　　Good people all, of every sort,
　　　　Give ear unto my song;
　　And if you find it wond'rous short,
　　　　It cannot hold you long.

In Islington there was a man,
  Of whom the world might say,
That still a godly race he ran,
  Whene'er he went to pray.

A kind and gentle heart he had,
  To comfort friends and foes,
The naked every day he clad,
  When he put on his clothes.

And in that town a dog was found,
  As many dogs there be,
Both mongrel, puppy, whelp, and hound,
  And curs of low degree.

This dog and man at first were friends;
  But when a pique began,
The dog, to gain some private ends,
  Went mad and bit the man.

Around from all the neighbouring streets
  The wond'ring neighbours ran,
And swore the dog had lost his wits,
  To bite so good a man.

The wound it seem'd both sore and sad
  To every Christian eye;
And while they swore the dog was mad,
  They swore the man would die.

But soon a wonder came to light,
  That show'd the rogues they lied;
The man recover'd of the bite,
  The dog it was that died.

Harry Graham (1874–1936)

Illustrated by 'G. H.' and Ridgewell

The Stern Parent

Father heard his Children scream,
So he threw them in the stream,
Saying as he drowned the third,
'Children should be seen, *not* heard!'

L'Enfant Glacé

When Baby's cries grew hard to bear
I popped him in the Frigidaire.
I never would have done so if
I'd known that he'd be frozen stiff.
My wife said: 'George, I'm so unhappé!
Our darling's now completely *frappé*!'

Robert Graves (1895–   )

A Grotesque

Dr Newton with the crooked pince-nez
Has studied in Vienna and Chicago,
Chess was his only relaxation.
And Dr Newman remained unperturbed
By every nastier manifestation
Of plutodemocratic civilization;
All that was cranky, corny, ill-behaved,
Unnecessarily askew, or orgiastic
Would creep unbidden to his side-door (hidden

Behind a poster in the Tube Station,
Nearly half-way up the moving-stairs),
Push its way in, to squat there undisturbed
Among box-files and tubular steel-chairs.
He was once seen at the Philharmonic Hall
Noting the reactions of two patients,
With pronounced paranoiac tendencies,
To old Dutch music. He appeared to recall
A tin of lozenges in his breast-pocket,
Put his hand confidently in –
And drew out a black imp, or sooterkin,
Six inches long, with one ear upside-down,
Licking at a vanilla ice-cream cornet –
Then put it back again with a slight frown.

W. Heath Robinson (1869–1944)

The New Diving Boat

((For those lacking sufficient courage to take the plunge)

High Tide

A. P. Herbert (1890–1971)

Plum's Dying Speech

From Two Gentlemen of Soho

Now popes and persons, majesties and powers,
Dominions, sunsets, Kings, and macaroons,
Violets, marigolds, and moonlight falling
Like children's kisses on the mountain top.
Dukes, ferns, and shellfish, and all gentle things
In the high argument of love suspended,
Firelight at evening and the dawn of day,
Redwings and walnuts, oak, mahogany,
Lancaster, York, great Salisbury and Monmouth,
Hereford, Leicester, Northumberland, and Kent,
King's Cross, St Pancras, Euston, Waterloo—
All noble-sounding and capacious words,
Come and be mourners at my funeral,
For I am in the vestibule of death.

    (Stabs self)

This is the gate and portal of my ending,
I think there doth not any word remain,
But silence and still quiet touch my lips
With the mute harmony of things unspoken.

I never was of that loud company
Which seek their harvest in a waste of words;
'Do' was my dictionary. And my sword
Leaped from the sheath ere I could mention it.

    (Stabs self. He falls — then sits up again perkily)

As you may see in some great orchestra
A little lonely fellow at the end
Sits by the cymbals, and the instruments
Thunder around him their tempestuous din, –
Flutes, horns, and oboes, harp and clarinet,
And the wild fiddles like the forest swaying
On Swedish mountains when the storm is high. –
But he, that could with one most royal clash
Startle the city and make all that music
Like the small twittering of birds appear,
Sits with his brasses, but doth make no sound
Till the conductor shall command him so.

    (Orchestra music stops)

And leaves his cymbals and goes home at last,
Still with no sound, nor kindly thanks, nor notice,
For the conductor hath forgotten him –
So sit I here and die without a word.

    (Stabs himself and falls back on the floor)

Dr Heinrich Hoffmann (1809–94)

The Story of Augustus

Illustrated by Quentin Blake

Augustus was a chubby lad;
Fat ruddy cheeks Augustus had;
And everybody saw with joy
The plump and hearty healthy boy.
He ate and drank as he was told,
And never let his soup get cold.
But one day, one cold winter's day,
He scream'd out — 'Take the soup away!
O take the nasty soup away!
I won't have any soup today.'

Next day, now, the picture shows
How lank and lean Augustus grows!
Yet, though he feels so weak and ill,
The naughty fellow cries out still —

'Not any soup for me, I say:
O take the nasty soup away!
I won't have any soup today.'

The third day comes: Oh what a sin!
To make himself so pale and thin.
Yet, when the soup is put on the table,
He screams, as loud as he is able, —
'Not any soup for me, I say:
O take the nasty soup away!
I won't have any soup today.'

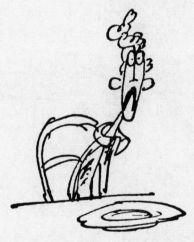

Look at him, now the fourth day's come!
He scarcely weighs a sugar-plum;
He's like a little bit of thread,
And on the fifth day, he was — dead!

Gerard Hoffnung (1925–59)

The Organ

The Horn

The Tenor

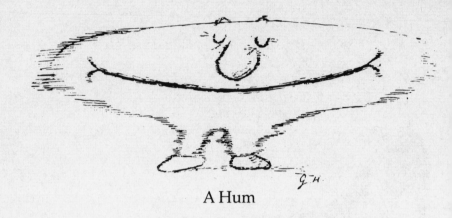

A Hum

Oliver Wendell Holmes (1809–94)
The Last Laugh

I wrote some lines once on a time
   In wondrous merry mood,
And thought, as usual, men would say
   They were exceeding good.

They were so queer, so very queer,
   I laughed as I would die;
Albeit, in the general way,
   A sober man am I.

I called my servant, and he came;
   How kind it was of him
To mind a slender man like me,
   He of the mighty limb!

'These to the printer,' I exclaimed,
   And, in my humorous way,
I added (as a trifling jest)
   'There'll be the devil to pay.'

He took the paper, and I watched,
   And saw him peep within;
At the first line he read, his face
   Was all upon the grin.

He read the next; the grin grew broad,
    And shot from ear to ear;
He read the third; a chuckling noise
    I now began to hear.

The fourth; he broke into a roar;
    The fifth; his waistband split;
The sixth; he burst five buttons off,
    And tumbled in a fit.

Ten days and nights, with sleepless eye,
    I watched that wretched man,
And since, I never dare to write
    As funny as I can.

A. E. Housman (1859–1936)

On the Death of a Female Officer of the Salvation Army

Illustrated by Tomi Ungerer

'Hallelujah!' was the only observation
That escaped Lieutenant-Colonel Mary Jane,
When she tumbled off the platform in the station,
And was cut in little pieces by the train.
    Mary Jane, the train is through yer!
    Hallelujah, Hallelujah!
We shall gather up the fragments that remain.

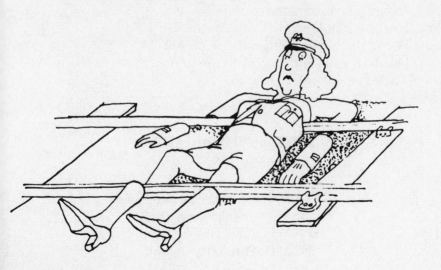

Ted Hughes (1930–)
My Uncle Dan

My Uncle Dan's an inventor, you may think that's very fine.
You may wish he was your Uncle instead of being mine —
If he wanted he could make a watch that bounces when it drops,
He could make a helicopter out of string and bottle tops
Or any really useful thing you can't get in the shops.
   But Uncle Dan has other ideas:
   The bottomless glass for ginger beers,
   The toothless saw that's safe for the tree,
   A special word for a spelling bee
   (like Lionocerangoutangadder),
   Or the roll-uppable rubber ladder,
   The mystery pie that bites when it's bit—
   My Uncle Dan invented it.
My Uncle Dan sits in his den inventing night and day.
His eyes peer down from his hair and beard like mice from a
     load of hay.
And does he make the shoes that will go walks without
     your feet?
A shrinker to shrink instantly the elephants you meet?
A carver that just carves from the air steaks cooked and
     ready to eat?
   No, no, he has other inventions—
   Only perfectly useless inventions:
   Glassless windows (they never break),
   A medicine to cure the earthquake,
   The unspillable screwed-down cup,
   The stairs that go neither down nor up,
   The door you simply paint on the wall –
   Uncle Dan invented them all.

Christopher Isherwood (1904–)
The Common Cormorant

     The common cormorant (or shag)
     Lays eggs inside a paper bag,
     You follow the idea, no doubt?
     It's to keep the lightning out.

But what these unobservant birds
Have never thought of, is that herds
Of wandering bears might come with buns
And steal the bags to hold the crumbs.

'ITMA' by Ted Kavanagh (1894–1958)

TOMMY HANDLEY: Hello folks. 'It's That Man Again' and what a man. My name today is on the tip of everyone's tongue and the toe of everyone's boot. Why, I can't go out in the open these days without people shouting 'Heil Itma'! Some say 'Good old Itma' and others 'There goes the old blast-furnace' or words to that effect. I have been evacuated now for three weeks — three weeks of high jinks and low pranks. We've been very busy in the Office of Twerps though — making out official forms and scribbling all over them, issuing orders one day and cancelling them the next. And the things we've written on the walls! Talk about one rood, pole or perch! My female staff have been extremely busy knitting me a pair of the most gorgeous galoshes you ever saw and now they're working on a surprise they're going to give me at Christmas — a shockproof waterproof and underproof Funfprotector. There's been no sign or sound of Funf during the week and I must admit that I'm seriously concerned when I fail to hear from him — especially at night. That's when I suffer badly from Funf-starvation.

Now let me see — what's been laid on my desk this morning. A duck egg, two dicarbicated cotton cow-cakes and a blue paper tied with red tape. I wonder what it can be? Ah — the plans of my secret broadcasting station. I must sit down to consider them.

Maurice Denham:	(dog yelping)
TOMMY HANDLEY:	Well muzzle mastaff that dog of mine in my chair again. Here, Isosceles. I'm the only one that's allowed to sleep in that chair.
Maurice Denham:	(as dog) Funf to you.
TOMMY HANDLEY:	Go and take your tail for a ta-ta. Now, I must examine these plans . . .

(*Hammering through wall*)

| TOMMY HANDLEY: | Nice quiet place this. |

(*Door opens*)

TOMMY HANDLEY:	Hello — what do you want? Oh – you're the man who's come to lay the telephone on.
MAN:	Oomph.
TOMMY HANDLEY:	Well get on with it. How long is it going to take you?
MAN:	Oomph.
TOMMY HANDLEY:	Can't you do it any quicker?
MAN:	Oomph — oomph.
TOMMY HANDLEY:	Nice chatty little fellow, isn't he?

(*Hammering continues*)

| TOMMY HANDLEY: | Make less noise there. I must have peace to consider this blueprint. |

(*Door opens*)

TOMMY HANDLEY:	Ah, good morning, Fusspot. Any letters this morning?
FUSSPOT:	Only one from my wife, sir.
TOMMY HANDLEY:	Your wife? Isn't she speaking to you?
FUSSPOT:	Oh sir, it's most enjoyable, most enjoyable. . .
TOMMY HANDLEY:	What is? Living with Mrs Fusspot? I'd rather eat iron filings.
FUSSPOT:	No, it's not that, sir. (*laughs*) She's left me!
TOMMY HANDLEY:	Well I'll sleep in my singlet! Left you?
FUSSPOT:	(*laughing*) Yes, sir, isn't it awful? She's gone back to London in a huff, sir.
TOMMY HANDLEY:	In a huff? Couldn't she get a cab?
FUSSPOT:	She says in her letter that you're a — you're a — (*laughs*) —

TOMMY HANDLEY:	I'm a what?
FUSSPOT:	You're a snake in the grass, sir.
TOMMY HANDLEY:	As long as she doesn't say I'm a toad in the hole, I'm all right.

(*Tramp of feet*)

TOMMY HANDLEY:	Here, get off my desk — you telephone tapper. And take your feet out of my ink-well.
FUSSPOT:	She says you're a Jack-in-office, sir, and a . . .
TOMMY HANDLEY:	Puss-in-boots and a pig-in-a-poke.
FUSSPOT:	She's a wonderful woman, sir. She's far too good for me.
TOMMY HANDLEY:	She frightened the life out of me.

(*Crash*)

TOMMY HANDLEY:	Now look what that automatic assassin's done. He's knocked over my aquarium and trod on my tiddlers. Can't you look where you're going?
MAN:	Oomph.
TOMMY HANDLEY:	I think he's hollow. Well Fusspot, you've got your freedom at last but don't get fresh with the fillies.
FUSSPOT:	I'll miss my Tou-Tou, sir — she's far too good for me.
TOMMY HANDLEY:	Well don't bring her back here — we've got all the wild animals we want on this farm. Send in Vodkin, will you? I must consider these plans. Now let me see — yes — the cowshed makes a grand studio and what a canteen! Ten times as big as any other room in the building.

(*Knock at door*)

TOMMY HANDLEY:	Come in!

(*Loud mooing of cows*)

FARMER JOLLOP:	Git on there, Strawberry. Git on Gladys. Eech-oop there, git on . . .

(*Mooing still louder*)

TOMMY HANDLEY:	Here, take those cows out of my office. Who sent them in here?
JOLLOP:	This be only way to pasture now, zur, since they're using cowshed for that danged wireless.
TOMMY HANDLEY:	Do you mean to say that every time they're milked they'll come through my office?
JOLLOP:	This be only way, zur.
TOMMY HANDLEY:	Well I'll be bunkered in the bulrushes! Here am I — the Minister of Aggravation with an office full of cows.
JOLLOP:	I'll soon clear 'em out, zur. Ech up Daphne — eel up there.

(*Loud mooing until door closes*)

TOMMY HANDLEY:	Nice quiet place this.

(*Door opens*)

VODKIN:	Oh, Mr Handmedown. It works, it works!
TOMMY HANDLEY:	What does? Our broadcasting station?
VODKIN:	No, the egg factory. It has exceeded all my cackle-ations.
TOMMY HANDLEY:	Tell me all about it, old cock.
VODKIN:	Every hen she lay two times, once in the morning and once at night.
TOMMY HANDLEY:	What, no matinees?
VODKIN:	At night the hen she sleeps, yes?
TOMMY HANDLEY:	Hen-variably.
VODKIN:	I switch the light and up she wakes. The cock he crow — the hen she lay. Then again she sleep. Again I switch the light and again she lay. Now a million eggs I have.
TOMMY HANDLEY:	I wish I had as many shillings.
VODKIN:	What are you going to do?
TOMMY HANDLEY:	I know — we'll sell 'em. Call 'em Itma eggs. The yolk of the century. Is our radio station ready?
VODKIN:	Oh yes, Mr Hanandegg.
TOMMY HANDLEY:	We'll get busy — we'll broadcast the Itma Egg programme right away. Well, folks,

the next part of the programme comes to you by courtesy of the Itma Egg Factory — the eggs with chick appeal.

ANNOUNCER: Allo, Ici Radio Twerpenburg, Défense de cracher.

(*Fanfare*)

ANNOUNCER: The Itma All-In Egg Programme.
CAVENDISH THREE: It's those eggs again
To put you on your legs again
Order 'em now.
And do not delay
Straight from the cow
They are fresh laid today,
It's those eggs again
The eggs that every grocer hates to sell —
So if you feel yeller and want a best smeller
Eat Itma and come right out of your shell.

ANNOUNCER: Good evening, everyone. Tonight the makers of Itma eggs — they're oh so strong and ever so shapely — bring you an omelette of 'armony with The Three Cacklers, Scrambled Sam the Double-yoked Yodeller, and Tommy Henlaid — the high cockalorum of comedy — accompanied by Billy Buff-Orpington and his Fowl-Fiddlers.

(*Fanfare*)

TOMMY HANDLEY: Hello, yolks — have you ever tried Itma eggs? They're all singing, all humming, and all-bumen. The only eggs that are all they're cracked up to be. You'll find the maker's name stamped on the blunt end and countersigned by the rooster on the sharp end. With every dozen we give away a gas mask. Itma eggs can be whipped but they can't be beaten. And now, Scrambled Sam will spread himself on a slice of toast.

Paul Jennings (1918–   )
Galoshes

I am having a *rapprochement* with galoshes
And some would say this heralds middle age;
Yes, sneering they would say
'Does he always wear *pince-nez*?
Old jossers wore galoshes when ladies' hats were cloches,
Ha! Woollen combinations are this dodderer's next stage!'
Well, let these people snigger
Just because my feet look bigger,
For, colossal in galoshes, they are dry among the sploshes;
A story that won't wash is this notion that galoshes,
So snug at slushy crossings, make a man a sloppy figure.
Oh, crossly, and still crosslier,
I have bought shoes even costlier
Which, still quite new, let water through before
    I've crossed the street:
There's nothing manly, I repeat,
In always having cold wet feet;
Galoshlessness is foolishness when sharply slants the sleet —
And I utterly refuse
The expression 'overshoes',
To make galoshes posher I would scorn this feeble ruse.
The word 'galosh' is strong, not weak,
It comes from *Kalopous*, the Greek
For 'cobbler's last', and thus it's classed with hero times antique.
Come, Muse, through slush and sleet dry-footed with me trip so
That I may praise galoshes in a *kalopous* calypso.
Oh, when swishing buses splash.
And the rush-hour masses clash
When it's marshy as molasses, how galoshes cut a dash!
It makes me quite impassioned
When they're dubbed unsmart, old-fashioned —
(For such, by gosh, the bosh is that's talked about galoshes)
Since the very finest leather
Is outsmarted altogether
By the classy, glossy polish of galoshes in such weather.

Come, galoshers, be assertive,
Drop that air discreet and furtive!

Let galosh shops' stocks be lavish
With designs and hues that ravish —
Men's galoshes black and British, but for ladies colours skittish
(And galoshes could make rings
Round those silly plastic things
Which tie up with clumsy strings)
Let us all have this *rapprochement* with galoshes
And see what health and happiness it brings!

Samuel Johnson (1709–84)

Hermit Hoar . . .

Hermit hoar, in solemn cell,
   Wearing out life's evening gray,
Smite thy bosom, Sage, and tell,
   What is bliss? And which the way?

Thus I spoke; and speaking sigh'd;
   Scarce repress'd the starting tear;
When the heavy sage reply'd,
   'Come, my lad, and drink some beer.'

John Keats (1795–1821)

From A Song of Myself

There was a naughty boy
   And a naughty boy was he
For nothing would he do
   But scribble poetry –
     He took
     An ink stand
     In his hand
     And a Pen
     Big as ten
     In the other,
     And away
     In a Pother
     He ran
     To the mountains
     And fountains

And ghostes
And Postes
And witches
And ditches
And wrote
In his coat
When the weather
Was cool.
Fear of gout
And without
When the weather
Was warm –
Och the charm
When we choose
To follow one's nose
To the north,
To the north,
To follow one's nose
To the north!

There was a naughty boy,
And a naughty boy was he,
He ran away to Scotland
The people for to see –
Then he found
That the ground
Was as hard,
That a yard
Was as long
That a song
Was as merry,
That a cherry
Was as red –
That lead
Was a weighty
That fourscore
Was as eighty.
That a door
Was as wooden
As in England –
So he stood in his shoes
And he wonder'd,

He wonder'd,
He stood in his shoes
And he wonder'd

Stephen Leacock (1869–1944)

The Awful Fate of Melpomenus Jones

Some people — not you nor I, because we are so awfully self-possessed — but some people, find great difficulty in saying good-bye when making a call or spending the evening. As the moment draws near when the visitor feels that he is fairly entitled to go away he rises and says abruptly, 'Well, I think I . . .' Then the people say, 'Oh, must you go now? Surely it's early yet!' and a pitiful struggle ensues.

I think the saddest case of this kind of thing that I ever knew was that of my poor friend Melpomenus Jones, a curate — such a dear young man, and only twenty-three! He simply couldn't get away from people. He was too modest to tell a lie, and too religious to wish to appear rude. Now it happened that he went to call on some friends of his on the very first afternoon of his summer vacation. The next six weeks were entirely his own — absolutely nothing to do. He chatted awhile, drank two cups of tea, then braced himself for the effort and said suddenly:

'Well, I think I . . .'

But the lady of the house said, 'Oh, no! Mr Jones, can't you really stay a little longer?'

Jones was always truthful. 'Oh, yes,' he said. 'Of course, I - er - can stay.'

'Then please don't go.'

He stayed. He drank eleven cups of tea. Night was falling. He rose again.

'Well now,' he said shyly, 'I think I really . . .'

'You must go?' said the lady politely. 'I thought perhaps you could have stayed to dinner . . .'

'Oh well, so I could, you know,' Jones said, 'if . . .'

'Then please stay, I'm sure my husband will be delighted.'

'All right,' he said feebly, 'I'll stay,' and he sank back into his chair, just full of tea, and miserable.

Papa came home. They had dinner. All through the meal Jones sat planning to leave at eight-thirty. All the family wondered whether Mr Jones was stupid and sulky, or only stupid.

After dinner mamma undertook to 'draw him out,' and showed him photographs. She showed him all the family museum, several gross of them — photos of papa's uncle and his wife, and mamma's brother and his little boy, an awfully interesting photo of papa's uncle's friend in his Bengal uniform, an awfully well-taken photo of papa's grandfather's partner's dog, and an awfully wicked one of papa as the devil for a fancy-dress ball.

At eight-thirty Jones had examined seventy-one photographs. There were about sixty-nine more that he hadn't. Jones rose.

'I must say good night now,' he pleaded.

'Say good night!' they said, 'why it's only half-'ast eight! Have you anything to do?'

'Nothing,' he admitted, and muttered something about staying six weeks, and then laughed miserably.

Just then it turned out that the favourite child of the family, such a dear little romp, had hidden Mr Jones's hat; so papa said that he must stay, and invited him to a pipe and a chat. Papa had the pipe and gave Jones the chat, and still he stayed. Every moment he meant to take the plunge, but couldn't. Then papa began to get very tired of Jones, and fidgeted and finally said, with jocular irony, that Jones had better stay all night, they could give him a shake-down. Jones mistook his meaning and thanked him with tears in his eyes, and papa put Jones to bed in the spare room and cursed him heartily.

After breakfast next day, papa went off to his work in the city, and left Jones playing with the baby, broken-hearted. His nerve was utterly gone. He was meaning to leave all day, but the thing had got on his mind and he simply couldn't. When papa came home in the evening he was surprised and chagrined to find Jones still there. He though to jockey him out with a jest, and said he thought he'd have to charge him for his board, he! he! The unhappy young man stared wildly for a moment, then wrung papa's hand, paid him a month's board in advance, and broke down and sobbed like a child.

In the days that followed he was moody and unapproachable. He lived, of course, entirely in the drawing-room, and the lack of air and exercise began to tell sadly on his health. He passed his time in drinking tea and looking at the photographs. He would stand for hours gazing at the photographs of papa's uncle's friend in his Bengal uniform — talking to it, sometimes swearing bitterly at it. His mind was visibly failing.

At length the crash came. They carried him upstairs in a raging delirium of fever. The illness that followed was terrible. He recognised no one, not even papa's uncle's friend in his Bengal uniform. At

times he would start up from his bed and shriek, 'Well, I think I . . .'
and then fall back upon the pillow with a horrible laugh. Then, again,
he would leap up and cry, 'Another cup of tea and more photographs!
More photographs! Har! Har!'

At length after a month of agony, on the last day of his vacation, he
passed away. They say that when the last moment came, he sat up in
bed with a beautiful smile of confidence playing upon his face, and
said, 'Well — the angels are calling me; I'm afraid I really must go
now. Good afternoon.'

And the rushing of his spirit from its prison-house was as rapid as a
hunted cat passing over a garden fence.

Edward Lear (1812–88)

The Owl and the Pussy-cat

The Owl and the Pussy-cat went to sea
   In a beautiful pea-green boat,
They took some honey, and plenty of money,
   Wrapped up in a five-pound note.
The Owl looked up to the stars above,
   And sang to a small guitar,
'O lovely Pussy! O Pussy, my love,
     What a beautiful Pussy you are,
       You are,
       You are!
     What a beautiful Pussy you are!'

Pussy said to the Owl, 'You elegant fowl!
   How charmingly sweet you sing!
O let us be married! too long we have tarried:
   But what shall we do for a ring?'
They sailed away, for a year and a day,
   To the land where the Bong-tree grows
   And there in a wood a Piggy-wig stood
     With a ring at the end of his nose,
       His nose,
       His nose,
     With a ring at the end of his nose.

'Dear Pig, are you willing to sell for one shilling
   Your ring?' Said the Piggy, 'I will.'
So they took it away, and were married next day
   By the Turkey who lives on the hill.
They dined on mince, and slices of quince,
   Which they ate with a runcible spoon;
And hand in hand, on the edge of the sand,
    They danced by the light of the moon,
     The moon,
     The moon,
    They danced by the light of the moon.

The Duck and the Kangaroo

Illustrated by David Farris

Said the Duck to the Kangaroo,
   'Good gracious! how you hop!
'Over the fields and the water too,
   'As if you never would stop!
'My life is a bore in this nasty pond,
'And I long to go out in the world beyond!
   'I wish I could hop like you!'
   Said the Duck to the Kangaroo.

'Please give me a ride on your back!'
   Said the Duck to the Kangaroo.
'I would sit quite still, and say nothing
     but "Quack!"
   'The whole of the long day through!
'And we'd go to the Dee, and the Jelly Bo Lee,
'Over the land, and over the sea; —
   'Please take me for a ride! O do!'
   Said the Duck to the Kangaroo.

Said the Kangaroo to the Duck,
   'This requires some little reflection;
'Perhaps on the whole it might bring me luck,
   'And there seems but one objection,
'Which is, if you'll let me speak so bold,
'Your feet are unpleasantly wet and cold,
   'And would probably give me the roo–
   'Matiz!' said the Kangaroo.

Said the Duck, 'As I sat on the rocks,
　'I have thought over that completely,
'And I bought four pairs of worsted socks
　'Which fit my web-feet neatly.
'And to keep out the cold I've bought a cloak,
'And every day a cigar I'll smoke,
　'All to follow my own dear true
　'Love of a Kangaroo!'

Said the Kangaroo, 'I'm ready!
'All in the moonlight pale;
'But to balance me well, dear Duck, sit steady!
'And quite at the end of my tail!'
So away they went with a hop and a bound,
And they hopped the whole world three
times round;
And who so happy, – O who,
As the Duck and the Kangaroo?

From The Story of the Four Little Children
Who Went Round the World

Illustrated by Edward Lear

Once upon a time, a long while ago, there were four little people whose names were

VIOLET,   SLINGSBY,   GUY,   and LION

and they all thought they should like to see the world. So they bought a large boat to sail quite round the world by sea, and then they were to come back on the other side by land. The boat was painted blue with green spots, and the sail was yellow with red stripes; and when they set off, they only took a small Cat to steer and look after the boat, besides an elderly Quangle-Wangle, who had to cook the dinner and make the tea; for which purposes they took a large kettle.

For the first ten days they sailed on beautifully, and found plenty to eat, as there were lots of fish, and they had only to take them out of the sea with a long spoon, when the Quangle-Wangle instantly cooked them, and the Pussy-cat was fed with the bones, with which she expressed herself pleased on the whole, so that all the party were very happy.

During the day-time, Violet chiefly occupied herself in putting salt-water into a churn, while her three brothers churned it violently, in the hope that it would turn into butter, which it seldom, if ever, did; and in the evening they all retired into the Tea-kettle, where they all managed to sleep very comfortably, while Pussy and the Quangle-Wangle managed the boat.

After a time they saw some land at a distance; and when they came to it, they found it was an island made of water quite surrounded by earth. Besides that, it was bordered by evanescent isthmusses with a great Gulf-stream running about all over it, so that it was perfectly beautiful, and contained only a single tree, 503 feet high.

When they had landed, they walked about, but found to their great surprise, that the island was quite full of veal-cutlets and chocolate-drops, and nothing else. So they all climbed up the single high tree to discover, if possible, if there were any people; but having remained on the top of the tree for a week, and not seeing anybody, they naturally concluded that there were no inhabitants, and accordingly when they came down, they loaded the boat with two thousand veal-cutlets and a million of chocolate drops, and these afforded them sustenance for more than a month, during which time they pursued their voyage with the utmost delight and apathy.

The Jumblies

They went to sea in a Sieve, they did,
　In a Sieve they went to sea:
In spite of all their friends could say,
On a winter's morn, on a stormy day,
　In a Sieve they went to sea!
And when the Sieve turned round and round,
And everyone cried, 'You'll all be drowned!'
They called aloud, 'Our Sieve ain't big,
But we don't care a button! we don't care a fig!
　In a Sieve we'll go to sea!'

Far and few, far and few,
  Are the lands where the Jumblies live;
Their heads are green, and their hands are blue,
  And they went to sea in a Sieve.

They sailed away in a Sieve, they did,
  In a Sieve they sailed so fast,
With only a beautiful pea-green veil
Tied with a riband by way of a sail,
  To a small tobacco-pipe mast;
And everyone said, who saw them go,
'O won't they be soon upset, you know!
For the sky is dark, and the voyage is long,
And happen what may, it's extremely wrong
  In a Sieve to sail so fast!'
    Far and few, far and few,
      Are the lands where the Jumblies live;
    Their heads are green, and their hands are blue,
      And they went to sea in a Sieve.

The water it soon came in, it did,
  The water it soon came in;
So to keep them dry, they wrapped their feet
In a pinky paper all folded neat,
  And they fastened it down with a pin.

And they passed the night in a crockery-jar,
And each of them said, 'How wise we are!
Though the sky be dark, and the voyage be long,
Yet we never can think we were rash or wrong,
   While round in our Sieve we spin!'
     Far and few, far and few,
       Are the lands where the Jumblies live;
       Their heads are green, and their hands are blue,
       And they went to sea in a Sieve.

And all night long they sailed away;
   And when the sun went down,
They whistled and warbled a moony song
To the echoing sound of a coppery gong,
   In the shade of the mountains brown.
'O Timballo! How happy we are,
When we live in a sieve and a crockery-jar,
And all night long in the moonlight pale,
We sail away with a pea-green sail,
   In the shade of the mountains brown!'
     Far and few, far and few,
       Are the lands where the Jumblies live;
       Their heads are green, and their hands are blue,
       And they went to sea in a Sieve.

They sailed to the Western Sea, they did,
   To a land all covered with trees,
And they bought an Owl, and a useful Cart,
And a pound of Rice, and a Cranberry Tart,
   And a hive of silvery Bees.
And they bought a Pig, and some green Jack-daws,
And a lovely Monkey with lollipop paws,
And forty bottles of Ring-Bo-Ree,
   And no end of Stilton Cheese.
     Far and few, far and few,
       Are the lands where the Jumblies live;
       Their heads are green, and their hands are blue,
       And they went to sea in a Sieve.

And in twenty years they all came back,
   In twenty years or more,
And everyone said, 'How tall they've grown!

For they've been to the Lakes, and the Torrible Zone,
   And the hills of the Chankly Bore;
And they drank their health, and gave them a feast
Of dumplings made of beautiful yeast;
And everyone said, 'If we only live,
We too will go to sea in a Sieve,—
   To the hills of the Chankly Bore!'
   Far and few, far and few,
     Are the lands where the Jumblies live;
    Their heads are green, and their hands are blue,
    And they went to sea in a Sieve.

Nonsense Botany

Bottlephorkia Spoonifolia

Smalltoothcombia Domestica

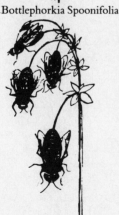

Bluebottlia Buzztilentia

Pollybirdia Singularis

Phattfacia Stupenda

Plumbunnia Nutritiosa

Manypeeplia Upsidownia

Guittara Pensilis

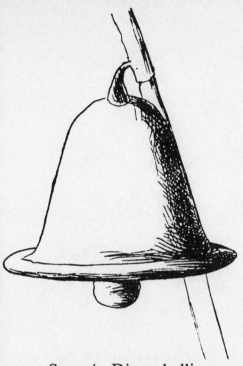

Stunnia Dinnerbellia

Tickia Orologica

Washtubbia Circularis

Tigerlillia Terribilis

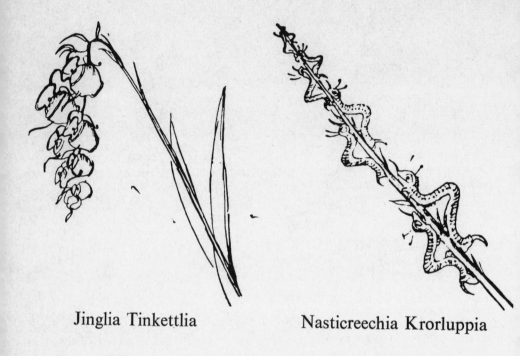

Jinglia Tinkettlia

Nasticreechia Krorluppia

Enkoopia Schickabbidia

Barkia Howlaloudia

John Lennon (1940–   )
I Sat Belonely down a Tree

I sat belonely down a tree,
humbled fat and small.
A little lady sing to me
I couldn't see at all.

I'm looking up and at the sky,
to find such wondrous voice.
Puzzly, puzzle, wonder why.
I hear but have no choice.

'Speak up, come forth, you ravel me,'
I potty menthol shout.
'I know you hiddy by this tree,'
But still she won't come out.

Such softly singing lulled me sleep,
an hour or two or so
I wakeny slow and took a peep
and still no lady show.

Then suddy on a little twig
I thought I see a sight,
A tiny little tiny pig,
that sing with all its might.

'I though you were a lady,'
I giggle – well I may.
To my surprise the lady,
got up — and flew away.

Dan Leno (George Galvin) (1860–1904)
From The Hampton Court Maze

It was very strange that I should first meet my wife in the Maze. I'd
never been in the Maze before (well I've never been out of one since). I
think every married man's a bit mazy, more or less. Well, to make a
long story thick, I was walking up and down, and after walking for

about two hours I found I hadn't moved; somehow or other I'd mislaid myself. I tried to find a side door at the back, but no. Then it struck me all of a lump that I was lost. Well it's dangerous to lose a person like me. So I began to cry, when someone over the other side of the hedge said, 'Don't cry, little boy, here's some nuts.' Oh, I was so pleased that I was found; and when I found it was a lady that was speaking, I shall never forget how I felt. I went all of a cold perspiration and I said, 'I ain't a little boy.' She said, 'I beg your pardon.' I said, 'You're welcome.' So one word got on to another; then she told me my name, and I told her hers. I asked her to go for a stroll when we got outside; she said she'd be delighted a lot, but how was she to know me? I said 'When we get out I'll cough twice.' So when I got out I coughed a lovely cough, and the man at the gate said, 'You've got hydrophobia.' I said, 'I beg to differ,' and then up came the girl. Oh, I was so bashful. I asked her to have some wine, so she ordered a pot of shandy gaff. I said, 'No, let's have two.' So I ordered two pots of gandy-shaff. I gave the waiter half a sovereign — no, let me see — fourpence; I get mixed a little. Then I ordered tea. I said, 'What will you have for tea?' She said, 'Anything you like.' So I ordered two plates of anything you like, and cruffins and mumpets. Oh, and we did have a game! I burnt her hand with a teaspoon and threw the watercress at the waiter, and she filled my cup with salt and I was sick. Oh, we did enjoy ourselves! Then we went home. But after leaving her I couldn't rest, nor eat my supper. I had to call my landlady up to sit with me a couple of hours. She said, 'Lor! Mr Pipkins, what's the matter with you?' and I told her I'd met my divinity. She said, 'Lor! have a mustard plaster on at once.' I said 'No, it's my sweetheart.' And I do believe if her mother hadn't have interfered we should have been happy. But! Lor, married life makes a man of you.

From Our Stoves

Where is there an article that will compel you to tell more lies than an egg? Do you know, I don't think we properly grasp eggs. There is something awfully artful about an egg — there is a mystery in it. Of course, there are three kinds of eggs — there is the new-laid egg (which is nearly extinct) — then there is the fresh egg, which is almost the same as the new-laid, but with an additional something about it that makes all the difference. Then comes The Egg; that is the egg I am talking about. That is the egg that causes all the trouble. It's only a little round white thing, but you can't tell what it's thinking about.

You daren't kick it, and you daren't drop it. It has got no face. You can't get it to laugh. You simply look at it and say, 'Egg!'

This morning a lady came in and said 'How do you sell eggs?' I said, 'As quickly as possible.' She walked out again.

C. S. Lewis (1898–1963)

Awake, My Lute!

I stood in the gloom of a spacious room
    Where I listened for hours (on and off)
To a terrible bore with a beard like a snore
    And a heavy rectangular cough,
Who discoursed on the habits of orchids and rabbits
    And how an electron behaves
And a way to cure croup which solidified soup
    In a pattern of circular waves;
Till I suddenly spied that what stood at his side
    Was a richly upholstered baboon
With paws like the puns in a poem of Donne's
    And a tail like a voyage to the Moon.
Then I whispered, 'Look out! For I very much doubt
    If your colleague is really a man.'
But the lecturer said, without turning his head,
    'Oh, that's only the Beverage plan!'
As one might have forseen, the whole sky became green
    At this most injudicious remark,
For the Flood had begun and we both had to run
    For our place in the queue to the Ark.
Then, I hardly know how (we were swimming by now),
    The sea got all covered with scum,
Made of publishers' blurbs and irregular verbs
    Of the kind which have datives in –um;
And the waves were so high that far up in the sky
    We saw the grand lobster, and heard
How he snorted, 'Compare the achievements of Blair
    With the grave of King Alfred the Third,
And add a brief note and if possible quote,
    And distinguish and trace and discuss
The probable course of a Methodist horse
    When it's catching a decimal bus.'

My answer was Yes. But they marked it N.S.,
    And a truffle fish grabbed at my toe,
And dragged me deep down to a bombulous town
    Where the traffic was silent and slow.
Then a voice out of heaven observed, 'Quarter past seven!'
    And I threw all the waves off my head,
For the voice beyond doubt was the voice of my scout,
    And the bed of that sea was my bed.

Vachel Lindsay (1879–1931)

The Daniel Jazz

A Negro's Interpretation of the Bible Story

Darius the Mede was a king and a wonder.
His eye was proud, and his voice was thunder.
He kept bad lions in a monstrous den.
He fed up the lions on Christian men.

Daniel was the chief hired man of the land,
He stirred up the jazz in the palace band.
He whitewashed the cellar. He shovelled in the coal.
And Daniel kept a-praying: 'Lord, save my soul.'
Daniel kept a-praying: 'Lord, save my soul.'
Daniel kept a-praying: 'Lord, save my soul.'

Daniel was the butler, swagger and swell,
He ran upstairs. He answered the bell.
And *he* would let in whoever came a-calling
Saints so holy, scamps so appalling.
'Old man Ahab leaves his card.
Elisha and the bears are a-waiting in the yard,
Here comes Pharaoh and his snakes a-calling,
Here comes Cain and his wife a-calling,
Shadrach, Meshach and Abednego for tea.
Here comes Jonah and the whale,
And the *sea*!
Here comes St Peter and his fishing-pole,
Here comes Judas and his silver a-calling,
Here comes old Beelzebub a-calling.'

And Daniel kept a-praying: 'Lord, save my soul.'
Daniel kept a-praying: 'Lord, save my soul.'
Daniel kept a-praying: 'Lord, save my soul.'

His sweetheart and his mother were Christians and meek,
They washed and ironed for Darius every week.
One Thursday he met them at the door;
Paid them as usual, but acted sore.
He said: 'Your Daniel is a dead little pigeon,
He's a good hard worker, but he talks religion.'
And he showed them Daniel in the lion's cage.
Daniel standing quietly, the lions in a rage.

His good old mother cried:-
'Lord, save him.'
And Daniel's tender sweetheart cried:-
'Lord, save him.'
And she was a golden lily in the dew.
And she was as sweet as an apple on the tree.
And she was as fine as a melon in the corn-field,
Gliding and lovely as a ship on the sea,
Gliding and lovely as a ship on the sea,

And she prayed to the Lord:-
'*Send* Gabriel. *Send* Gabriel.'

King Darius said to the lions:-
'Bite Daniel. Bite Daniel.
Bite him. Bite him. Bite him.'

Thus roared the lions:-
'We want Daniel, Daniel, Daniel.
We want Daniel, Daniel, Daniel.
Grrrrrrrrrrrr
Grrrrrrrrrrrr.'

And Daniel did not frown,
Daniel did not cry.
He kept on looking at the sky.

And the Lord said to Gabriel:-
'Go chain the lions down,
Go chain the lions down,
Go chain the lions down,
Go chain the lions down,'
And *Gabriel* chained the lions,
And *Gabriel* chained the lions,
And *Gabriel* chained the lions,
And Daniel got out of the den,
And Daniel got out of the den,
And Daniel got out of the den.
And Darius said: 'You're a Christian child,'
Darius said: 'You're a Christian child,'
Darius said: 'You're a Christian child,'
And gave him his job again,
And gave him his job again,
And gave him his job again.

Hugh Lofting (1886–1947)

From Gub Gub's Book (1932)

'Well, to go back to Patricia Portly. She helped me a great deal in trying out the best foods for a writer to work on. Her drawing-room was quite famous; and only the most refined pigs were invited to her parties. It was a pleasing sight to see her lolling on a couch surrounded by pigs of importance, pigs whose names were known everywhere, pigs who had really done things. I have quite a piece about her in my book. For she too made a name for herself in the History of Food Discovery. Yes indeed, she will be known to future students as the Inventor of Food Perfumes. A real pioneer, you might say. At every one of her parties she wore a different perfume: sometimes it was prune-juice; sometimes essence of caraway seeds; or nutmeg or barley broth; and she had one that I thought was particularly lovely, a mixture of vanilla and horse-radish — very delicate. But perhaps her greatest work of art in this kind of invention was first made public when she got married. She lay awake many nights trying to think up a new scent to be used at her wedding. You see she wanted a nosegay and—'

'A nosebag, you mean,' Jip put in with another grunt.

'She wanted a nosegay,' Gub-Gub went on, 'which would be something that had never been used by a bride before. And finally she decided on a bunch of Italian Forget-me-nots.'

'I never heard of the flower,' said Too-Too.

'Well, they're not exactly flowers,' said Gub-Gub. 'They are those long green onions that come in the Spring. You see the very refined pig society in which Patricia moved did not like to call them onions. So they changed the name to Italian Forget-me-nots. They became very fashionable after that and were nearly always used at pig weddings. Patricia's wedding was a very grand affair. The only thing that spoiled it, slightly, was that some of the guests instead of throwing ordinary rice at the happy couple, threw rice puddings. They meant well, thinking that the bride and groom would like cooked rice better than raw. But I must say it *was* a little untidy.'

Patricia Portly, 'The Venus of the Berkshires'

Archibald MacLeish (1892—   )

Mother Goose's Garland

Around, around the sun we go:
The moon goes round the earth.
We do not die of death:
We die of vertigo.

Walter de la Mare (1873–1956)

Green

There was an old grocer of Goring
Had a butter assistant named Green,
Who sank through a hole in the flooring
And never was afterwards seen.
   Did he look in his cellar?
   Did he miss the poor fellow?
   Not at all. Quite phlegmatic,
   He retired to an attic,
And there watched the moon in her glory o'er
           Goring—
A sight not infrequently seen.

The Bards

My aged friend, Mrs Wilkinson,
   Whose mother was a Lambe,
Saw Wordsworth once, and Coleridge, too,
   One morning in her p'ram.

Birdlike the bards stooped over her—
   Like fledgling in a nest:
And Wordsworth said, 'Thou harmless babe!'
   And Coleridge was impressed.

The pretty thing gazed up and smiled,
   And softly murmured, 'Coo!'
William was then aged sixty-four
   And Samuel sixty-two.

Don Marquis (1878–1937)

the coming of archy

The circumstances of archy's first appearance are narrated in the
following extract from the Sun Dial column of the New York *Sun*.

Dobbs Ferry possesses a rat which slips out of his lair at night and runs a typewriting machine in a garage. Unfortunately, he has always been interrupted by the watchman before he could produce a complete story.

It was at first thought that the power which made the typewriter run was a ghost, instead of a rat. It seems likely to us that it was both a ghost and a rat. Mme Blavatsky's ego went into a white horse after she passed over, and someone's personality has undoubtedly gone into this rat. It is an era of belief in communications from the spirit land.

And since this matter had been reported in the public prints and seriously received we are no longer afraid of being ridiculed, and we do not mind making a statement of something that happened to our own typewriter only a couple of weeks ago.

We came into our room earlier than usual in the morning, and discovered a gigantic cockroach jumping about upon the keys.

He did not see us, and we watched him. He would climb painfully upon the framework of the machine and cast himself with all his force upon a key, head downward, and his weight and the impact of the blow were just sufficient to operate the machine, one slow letter after another. He could not work the capital letters, and he had a great deal of difficulty operating the mechanism that shifts the paper so that a fresh line may be started. We never saw a cockroach work so hard or perspire so freely in all our lives before. After about an hour of this frightfully difficult literary labour he fell to the floor exhausted, and we saw him creep feebly into a nest of the poems which are always there in profusion.

Congratulating ourself that we had left a sheet of paper in the machine the night before so that all this work had not been in vain, we made an examination, and this is what we found:

expression is the need of my soul
i was once a vers libre bard
but i died and my soul went into the body of a cockroach
it has given me a new outlook upon life
i see things from the under side now
thank you for the apple peelings in the wastepaper basket
but your paste is getting so stale i cant eat it
there is a cat here called mehitabel i wish you would have
removed she nearly ate me the other night why dont she
catch rats that is what she is supposed to be for
there is a rat here she should get without delay
most of these rats here are just rats
but this rat is like me he has a human soul in him

he used to be a poet himself
night after night i have written poetry for you
on your typewriter
and this big brute of a rat who used to be a poet
comes out of his hole when it is done
and reads it and sniffs at it
he is jealous of my poetry
he used to make fun of it when we were both human
he was a punk poet himself
and after he has read it he sneers
and then he eats it

i wish you would have mehitabel kill that rat
or get a cat that is onto her job
and i will write you a series of poems showing how things look
to a cockroach
that rats name is freddy
the next time freddy dies i hope he wont be a rat
but something smaller i hope i will be a rat
in the next transmigration and freddy a cockroach
i will teach him to sneer at my poetry then
dont you ever eat any sandwiches in your office
i havent had a crumb of bread for i dont know how long
or a piece of ham or anything but apple parings
and paste leave a piece of paper in your machine
every night you can call me archy

aesop revised by archy

a wolf met a spring
lamb drinking
at a stream
and said to her
you are the lamb
that muddied this stream
all last year
so that i could not get
a clean fresh drink
i am resolved that
this outrage

shall not be enacted again
this season
i am going to kill you
just a moment
said the lamb
i was not born last
year so it could not
have been i
the wolf then pulled
a number of other
arguments as to why the lamb
should die
but in each case the lamb
pretty innocent that she was
easily proved
herself guiltless
well well said the wolf
enough of argument
you are right and i am wrong
but i am going to eat
you anyhow
because i am hungry
stop exclamation point
cried a human voice
and a man came over
the slope of the ravine
vile lupine marauder
you shall not kill that
beautiful and innocent
lamb for i shall save her
exit the wolf
left upper entrance
snarling
poor little lamb
continued our human hero
sweet tender little thing
it is well that i appeared
just when i did
it makes my blood boil
to think of the fright
to which you have been

subjected in another
moment i would have been
too late come home with me
and the lamb frolicked
about her new found friend
gambolling as to the sound
of a wordsworthian tabor
and leaping for joy
as if propelled by a stanza
from william blake
these vile and bloody wolves
went on our hero
in honest indignation
they must be cleared out
of the country
the meads must be made safe
for sheepocracy
and so jollying her along
with the usual human hokum
he led her to his home
and the son of a gun
did not even blush when
they passed the mint bed
gently he cut her throat
all the while inveighing
against the inhuman wolf
and tenderly he cooked her
and lovingly he sauced her
and meltingly he ate her
and piously he said a grace
thanking his gods
for their bountiful gifts to him
and after dinner
he sat with his pipe
before the fire meditating
on the brutality of wolves
and the injustice of
the universe
which allows them to harry
poor innocent lambs
and wondering if he
had not better

write to the papers
for as he said
for gods sake cant
something be done about it
        archy

Roger McGough (1937–   )

From Sporting Relations

Uncle Terry was a skydiver.
He liked best
the earth spread out beneath him
like a springcleaned counterpane.
The wind his safety net.

He free fell every day
and liked it so much
he decided to stay.
And they say he's still there
sunbathing in the air.

He sleeps each night
tucked up in moonlight
wakes at dawn
and chases clouds.

Living   off   the   food   birds   bring

Uncle   Terry   on   the   wing

away   from   it   all

dizzy   with   joy.

Uncle Jason, and ace in the Royal Flying Corps
grew up and old into a terrible borps.
He'd take off from tables to play the Great Worps
stretch out his arms and crash to the florps.

His sister, an exSister (now rich) of the Porps,
would rorps forps morps: 'Encorps! Encorps!'

Spike Milligan (1918–   )

Main characters from The Goon Show

Eccles

(The Original Goon)

Born 1863. Only child of Ethel Cox, Virgin birth. Educated at Convent till age 7 — end of education. Has had 18,312 interviews for jobs. Has never been employed. Spends his days walking around saying 'Hello dere' to anyone who will listen. Wears a 33-year-old Burton suit. Is occasionally used by the Metropolitan Police for target practice. Was once painted by Augustus John from head to foot with whitewash. Likes children. Children like him. His economy drives consist of wearing only one sock. Was the personal friend of a brewer's dray. Was Home Secretary for 3 days — until the printing error was discovered. Lives near 29 Scrot Lane, Balham. Clubs: none. Recreations: walking around saying 'Hello dere' to anyone who will listen.

Bluebottle

(A cardboard cut-out liquorice and string hero)

'Ye he he! Heuheuheuheuheu he!'
A hot sweet bag of dolly mixtures plus an electric twit for Christmas persuaded me to append my signature to the foregoing, whatever that means, (Thinks: I wonder what that means).

Mr Henry Crun

(A thin ancient and inventor)

'Mnk — grnk — mnk — mnk — grmp.'
(Persistent questioning failed to refresh Mr Crun's memory as to the identity of Mr Henry Crun, beyond the remark, 'Henry Crun? Mnk — isn't that the name of — mnk — Henry Crun?')

Miss Minnie Bannister

(Spinster of the Parish)

Although she refused to be quoted directly, some Sanders-style flattery induced Miss Bannister to reveal that she had once danced the

Can-Can at the Windmill Theatre, and that in the naughty nineties she had been 'the darling of Roper's Light Horse'. She also hinted at a former passionate involvement with a bounder named Bloodnok. When pressed, however, she screamed and referred all further questions to her spokesman and companion of honour, Mr Henry Crun.

Major Dennis Bloodnok, Ind. Arm. Rtd.

(Military idiot, coward and bar)

Born 1867 and 1880, Sandhurst NAAFI. Served in S. African war — taken prisoner on first day under strange circumstances. Released by Boers after 3 days as being 'unreliable'. Spent the rest of the war in the Pay Corps. Large sums of money were in his keeping. They were never traced. Transferred to Aldershot Southern Command as Quartermaster General — was responsible for 30,000 rupeesworth of stores. They were never traced. Military Police traced *him* to Rangoon, where he was found wearing false testicles in a Freak Show. Cashiered. Married the Hon. Mrs Scrack-Thing. Divorced, Rejoined Army under an assumed height as Florence Bloodnok; served 1 year in ATS. His disguise became known when he reported a sailor for molesting him in an air-raid shelter. Using his position as a mason, he re-joined the Army as a Major; he saw action and suffered wounds in the bedroom of Mrs Madge Feel, World War II — he was found hiding in a hut near Quetta, where he swore a solemn oath that he was an eccentric Hindu fakir who had gone white with fear. Cashiered for the 7th time — a world military record. Wearing a stocking mask, he rejoined the British Army as a Chinaman. Using masonic connections he became a Major again. Clubs: Anyone. Recreations: Piccadilly Circus. Hobbies: The Indian Army. Agent: Miss M. Bannister.

The Telephone

(With Larry Stephens)

ORCHESTRA:	*Bloodnok Theme*
BLOODNOK:	Oughgh! Aheheheheheh! Oucoucghgh! Aggoi-eigh! Aheheheheh! Well, I can't sit here all day.
ABDUL:	Sahib — Sahib — a Palladium-type-comic-type gentleman has just collapsed in a heap outside.
BLOODNOK:	I know — I tripped over that heap myself only this morning. I'll be glad when we're mechanized. Now lift up his wig and let's have a look at him.

SEAGOON:	(*groans*)
BLOODNOK:	Steady lad! Fan him with a thermometer, and put a copy of 'The Lancet' under his head.
SEAGOON:	(*groans*)
ABDUL:	Oh, goodness gracious, he is seriously unconscious, Major.
BLOODNOK:	No wonder — I'll just lift that heavy wallet off him (*quick counting*), no wonder, there were forty pounds pressing on his chest. Now we'll just restore the circulation in his arms with the toad ointment.
SEAGOON:	(*groans*)
BLOODNOK:	Just put this pen in his hand and run it lightly over this cheque, there —
SEAGOON:	Ah, oh, where am I?
BLOODNOK:	In the red.
SEAGOON:	Thank heavens — a British bank manager.
BLOODNOK:	He's delirious. Hold him down while I force this brandy between my lips.
SOUND EFFECT:	(*bubbling*)
BLOODNOK:	Yes — you look much better now, lad.
SEAGOON:	I'm looking for the inventor of the telephone.
BLOODNOK:	Ah, that's Crun. Henry Crun — so you're looking for that cool high-stepping fool, are you? Him and his sensual Caucasian knee-dancing — that's how he tempted poor Minnie away from me — Oh, Min!
SEAGOON:	Come now, Major, Dennis, please — dry your tears on this marble statue of a handkerchief.
BLOODNOK:	Thank you. Poor Min — abducted in the prime of her twilight. It's a long story — I remember it all started on the road to Mandalay — where the flying fishes play — and oh!
SEAGOON:	Yes yes yes yes — but that's your pigeon.
BLOODNOK:	So it is! How did it get out? Abdul, take this pigeon away and bring me a clothes-brush.

The Skate

'Tis sad to relate
That skate cannot skate!
In the sea, they lie on the bottom.
They lie quite still
In waters chill
Until a fisherman's got 'em!

A very sad fate
for the non-skating skate.

Chorus: Rule Britannia, etc. etc.

Adrian Mitchell (1932–   )

The Apeman's Hairy Body Song

Happy to be hairy
Happy to be hairy
When the breezes tickle
The hairs of my body

Happy to be hairy
Happy to be hairy
Next best thing
To having feathers

Monty Python —
Graham Chapman, John Cleese, Terry Gilliam, Eric Idle, Terry Jones, Michael Palin
From The Brand New Monty Python Bok (1973)

Rat Recipes

Rat pie:

Take four medium-sized rats and lay them on the chopping board.
Having first made sure the chopper is freshly sharpened, raise it as
high above the first rat as you can. Make sure that the rat's neck is well

exposed, then bring the chopper down with as much force as possible onto the neck or head of the rat. Then cook it in a pie.

Rat soufflé:

Make sure that the rat's squeals are not audible from the street, particularly in areas where the Anti-Soufflé League and similar do-gooders are out to persecute the innocent pleasures of the table. Anyway, cut the rat down and lay it on the chopping-board. Raise the chopper high above your head, with the steel glinting in the setting sun, and then bring it down—wham!—with a vivid crunch—straight across the taut neck of the terrified rodent, and make it into a soufflé.

Bits of rat hidden under a chair:

This isn't so much a recipe as a bit of advice in the event of members of the Anti-Soufflé League or its simpering lackeys breaking into your flat. Your wife (or a friend's) should engage the pusillanimous toadies from the League in conversation, perhaps turning the chat to the price of corn and the terrible damage inflicted by all kinds of rodents on personal property, and rats attacking small babies (this always takes the steam out of them) and you should have time to get any rat-bits safely out of sight. Incidentally do make sure that your current copy of *The Rat Gourmet* hasn't been left lying around, otherwise all will be in vain, and the braying hounds of the culinary killjoys will be un-leashed upon the things you cherish: your chopping-board, the chopper caught in the blood-red glare of the fading sun. Bring it down —crunch! The slight splintering of tiny spinal column under the keen metal! The last squeal and the death twitches of the helpless rat!

From Norman Henderson's Diary

Edited by Eric Henderson

Thursday March 22nd

At breakfast I had an innermost thought. How would horses run if they only had two legs, one at each end? A sort of rumba I suppose. Depressed me all morning.

Lunched with Duncan (Sandys) Heathcoat (Amory) and Reggie (Maudling) at Beefsteak. Duncan says Lord Chatsworth (Minister of Defence) is finished and must go (Lord C. had at this point been dead for over four months-ed.) Reggie agreed but said we *must* wait till after bye-elections (Nov. 14th).

3 o'clock. Cabinet meeting. P.M. not looking at all well. Pale and drawn and large hole in top of head. Also cries a lot. Asked me what I thought about cheese. What could I say? I replied that it was reliable enough stuff but that he should not count on it in an emergency. He seemed satisfied by this but Barbara (Windsor) thought it v. funny. She is a nice enough lady but must be a risk at the Board of Trade. Eventually meeting finished. Sad to see PM in this state. Just yodels to himself and makes faces in mirror. Also incontinent. And yet he is the best man we have! I was also surprised to find how easy it had been to get into a Cabinet meeting. A lot of foreigners there too.

Met Harold (Macmillan) and Lady Violet (Bonham-Carter) at Moo-Cow in Greek Street. Harold said crisis was on us but felt it best to keep it from nation in case they got annoyed. Baited waitress.

Tea at the Menuhins. A lot of fighting as usual. Took taxi home in nude but was involved in an accident with a lorry in Oxford Street. Was quite badly hurt and had to travel in ambulance to hospital. Died before we got there though.

Friday March 23rd

Nothing much. Funeral arranged for tomorrow. Rather depressed.

Saturday March 24th

Service at St Thomas, Belgravia. Then on to the cemetery. Buried about 11.15 a.m.

Edwin Morgan (1920–   )
The Computer's First Christmas Card

> jollymerry
> hollyberry
> jollyberry
> merryholly
> happyjolly
> jollyjelly
> jellybelly
> bellymerry
> hollyheppy
> jollyMolly
> marryJerry

merryHarry
hoppyBarry
heppyJarry
bobbyheppy
berryjorry
jorryjelly
moppyjelly
Mollymerry
Jerryjolly
bellyboppy
jarryhoppy
hollymoppy
Barrymerry
Jarryhappy
happyboppy
boppyjolly
jollymerry
merrymerry
merrymerry
merryChris
asmerryasa
Chrismerry
asMERRYCHR
YSANTHEMUM

Ogden Nash (1902–71)

The Poultries

Let's think of eggs.
They have no legs.
Chickens come from eggs,
But they have legs.
The plot thickens;
Eggs come from chickens,
But have no legs under 'em.
What a conundrum!

Thoughts Thought While Resting Comfortably in Phillips House, Massachusetts General Hospital, Overlooking the Charles River

Something, probably diet, seems to have stunted my mental
    growth,
I can't remember the difference between a valedictorian and
    a valetudinarian and I suspect that I am both.
In church when confessing my misdeeds, which I am truly
    distraught to have done,
I begin with those things I have done that I ought not to
    have done instead of those things I have left undone
    that I ought to have done.
Sometimes I spell sex s-e-c-k-s, not to be humorous,
Just because I feel it must be plural, it has become so
    numerous.
Problems of terminology grow more and more knotty;
I had just learned to say judo instead of jujitsu when it
    suddenly turned into karate.
I can't seem to get in step;
I know that a policeman is now fuzz instead of cop, but
    which does that knowledge make me, hip or hep?
I had just straightened out Guinea and Guiana,
And up popped Ghana.
My mind obviously needs renewal;
Come cosset me with posset, comfort me with comfits,
    refuel me with gruel.

There, that's better, now my mind takes a spry turn,
I remember the difference between a *pas de deux* and a
    padishah, padishah means great king or emperor and
    pas de deux means Now it's my turn.
I would be completely recovered but for a recent
    disappointment suffered when I distinctly heard
    Ed Sullivan announce the appearance of a group of
    Spanish dentures;
When they turned out to be Spanish dancers I asked the
    nurse to switch to a film about a dedicated nurse
    beset by topers and wenchers.

The Private Dining-room

Miss Rafferty wore taffeta,
Miss Cavendish wore lavender.
We ate pickerel and mackerel
And other lavish provender.

Miss Cavendish was Lalage,
Miss Rafferty was Barbara.
We gobbled pickled mackerel
And broke the candelabara,
Miss Cavendish in lavender,
In taffeta, Miss Rafferty,
The girls in taffeta lavender,
And we, of course, in mufti.

Miss Rafferty wore taffeta,
The taffeta was lavender,
Was lavend, lavender, lavenderest,
As the wine improved the provender.
Miss Cavendish wore lavender,
The lavender was taffeta.
We boggled mackled pickerel,
And bumpers did we quaffeta.
And Lalage wore lavender,
And lavender wore Barbara,
Rafferta taffeta Cavender Lavender
Barbara abracadabra.

Miss Rafferty in taffeta,
Grew definitely raffisher.
Miss Cavendish in lavender
Grew less and less stand-offisher.

With Lalage and Barbara
We grew a little pickereled,
We ordered Mumm and Roederer
Because the bubbles tickereled
But lavender and taffeta
Were gone when we were soberer.
I haven't thought for thirty years
Of Lalage and Barbara.

The Pig

The pig, if I am not mistaken,
Supplies us sausage, ham, and bacon.
Let others say his heart is big —
I call it stupid of the pig.

The Kangaroo

O Kangaroo, O Kangaroo,
Be grateful that you're in the zoo,
And not transmuted by a boomerang
To zestful tangy Kangaroo meringue.

Flann O'Brien (1911–66)

From 'The Best of Myles na Gopaleen'

The Dublin Waama League's Escort Service

(WAAMA = Writers, Actors, Artists, Musicians Association)

Our Service Explained

Here is how it happened. The WAAMA League has had on its hands
for some time past a horde of unemployed ventriloquists who have
been beseeching us to get them work. These gentlemen have now
been carefully trained and formed in a corps to operate this new escort
service.

Supposing you are a lady and so completely dumb that the dogs in
the street do not think you are worth growling at. You ring up the
WAAMA League and explain your trouble. You are pleased by the
patient and sympathetic hearing you get. You are instructed to be in
attendance at the foyer of the Gate Theatre that evening, and to look
out for a tall, distinguished-looking gentleman of military bearing
attired in immaculate evening dress. You go. You meet him. He
advances towards you smiling, ignoring all the other handsome
baggages that litter the place. In an instant his moustaches are brushing
your lips.

'I trust I have not kept you waiting, Lady Charlotte,' he says
pleasantly. What a delightfully low, manly voice!

'Not at all, Count,' you answer, your voice being the tinkle of silver bells. 'And what a night it is for Ibsen. One is in the mood, somehow. Yet a translation can never be quite the same. Do you remember that night . . . in Stockholm . . . long ago?'

The Secret

The fact of the matter is, of course, that you have taken good care to say nothing. Your only worry throughout the evening is to shut up and keep shut up completely. The trained escort answers his own manly questions in a voice far pleasanter than your own unfeminine quack, and gives answers that will astonish the people behind for their brilliance and sparkle.

There are escorts and escorts according to the number of potatoes you are prepared to pay . . .

The Myles na Gopaleen Catechism of Cliché

What happens to blows at a council meeting?
It looks as if they might be exchanged.
What does pandemonium do?
It breaks loose.
Describe its subsequent dominion.
It reigns.
How are allegations dealt with?
They are denied.
Yes, but then you are weakening, Sir. Come how, how are they denied?
Hotly.
What is the mean temperature of an altercation, therefore?
Heated.
What is the behaviour of a heated altercation?
It follows.
What happens to order?
It is restored.
Alternatively, what does the meeting do in disorder?
Breaks up.
In what direction does the meeting break in disorder?
Up.
In what direction should I shut?
Up.

Ann O'Connor (?—)

Rhubarb Ted

I knew a funny little man
His name was Rhubarb Ted;
They called him that because he wore
Rhubarb on his head.

I'd grown so used to this strange sight,
The cause I did not seek;
But then one day to my surprise,
I saw he wore a leek.

I asked him if he'd please explain,
And let me know the reason;
He said, 'I'm wearing leek because
Rhubarb's out of season!'

Philip O'Connor (1916–)

I

Captain Busby put his beard in his mouth and sucked it, then took it
out and spat on it then put it in and sucked it then walked on down the
street thinking hard. Suddenly he put his wedding-ring in his trilby
hat and put the hat on a passing kitten. Then he carefully calculated
the width of the pavement with a pair of adjustable sugar-tongs. This
done he knitted his brows. Then he walked on thinking hard.

II

Captain Busted Busby frowned hard at a passing ceiling and fixed his
eye upon a pair of stationary taxis. Suddenly he went up to one of
them and addressed himself to the driver. He discharged his socks
and continued whistling. The taxi saluted but he put up with it, and
puckered a resigned mouth and knitted a pair of thoughtful eye-
brows.

III

M. looking out of his window with purple curtains saw Captain Busby thoughtfully chewing a less impatient portion of his walking-stick unostentatiously against a lamp-post. The road was blue but Captain Busby seemed a very dark green with ivory face (for it was night time). He frowned. He looked up to the top of the rapidly emptying street. He cut his hair slowly. He looked at the bottom of the street. He made rapid measurements with a pair of adjustable sugar-tongs. These he afterwards secreted in his trousers. He then flew into his friend's apartment through the willingly opened window.

IV

Marcella waited for her lover outside a public house known to both of them. Immediately Captain Busby appeared holding a woman in his arms. This wasn't true thought Marcella carefully, and was relieved to see that God had thrown a lamp-post at the Captain, temporarily disabling him.

V

He arranged himself in sugar and put himself in his bath
and prepared to breath his last.
his four bottles lay grouped around him
do your duty in this world and gather dividends from the
dog thrown at you
goodbye my children
and he died and they huskily nailed down his coffin
and put it in ten feet of sod
and grouped around him reading the will
and indeed and forever would he be
to them
just dad

VI

Mother lay crying in the withdrawing room
bitterly bewailing cruel fate who with a flick of his pen

had so completely shattered the even tenor of her ways
sobbed upon the brick platform shaking her fist at every
    porter who passed
declaring cruel fate who with a flick of his pen
had so cruelly broken
the even tenor of her ways.

VII

she considered the porter with the cap on the side of his head
    fitfully
who had squandered his sweet-peas upon her
who had ridden every train and blown all whistles
to feast his evil frontal eyes on her to break the even tenor
    of her ways
she shunted her back to him
she put on her large black hat with insolent vulgarity
and deliberately smirked into his face

he was busy
he was doing his duty
he rattled the cans
he gave out composed answers to the backchat following
    his curt commands
he went on with his duty forgetting
that he had broken the even tenor of her ways
She walked thoughtfully upon a sugar-box
and would there and then have harangued the station
    officials to compel the attention of the porter

but he did not
but he could not
but he did not
and could not should as he had broken the even tenor
    of her ways
she thrust a carrot into his face
he gravely took it and handed it without moving a muscle
    of his face
to the dominant personality of the station
the station master himself

events moved indefatigably to their long-awaited climax
the station master seized the carrot and conveyed it to
    a drawer
reserved for matters of importance
and seizing a document asserting his credentials and
    authority
motored along the platform and alighted at the lady

madam he said coldly
your carrot is in the drawer
pray come for it or suitable measures will be taken to
    enforce
the union of yourself and the personality
who broke the even tenor of your ways

Lightning juggled above the station portraying its grim
battlements
thunder crashed upon the assembled people
she threw three flashes of self-possessed rays
at him from her large radiant eyes
she ran to the drawer refusing the automobile
she snatched abruptly at the carrot
scenting with inexorable female intuition the precise
    position afforded it by reason of its pre-eminent
    significance
she ran from the house like a bitten wounded thing
and fell laughing upon the station master who had
    broken
the even
tenor of her ways

Brian Patten (1946–   )

Little Johnny's Confession

This morning
    being rather young and foolish
    I borrowed a machinegun my father
    had left hidden since the war, went out,
    and eliminated a number of small enemies.
    Since then I have not returned home.

This morning
    swarms of police with tracker dogs
    wander about the city
    with my description printed
    on their minds, asking:
    'Have you seen him,
    He is seven years old,
    likes Pluto, Mighty Mouse
    and Biffo the Bear,
    have you seen him, anywhere?'

This morning
    sitting along in a strange playground,
    muttering You've blundered You've blundered
    over and over to myself
    I work out my next move
    but cannot move;
    the trackerdogs will sniff me out,
    they have my lollypops.

Mervyn Peake (1911–68)

O Love! O Death! O Ecstasy!

O Love! O Death! O Ecstasy!
O rhubarb burning by the sea!
O day of nought — O night of doubt
Beneath the moon's marmorial mout
Ah pity, pity me!

A voice across the coughing brine
Has sewn your spirit into mine,
O love! it is for me to die
Upon your bosom noisily.

Along the cold, regurting
Shore we passed,
My arm around her irritating
Wasp-like waist
She likes it so.

O HERE IT IS AND THERE IT IS...

Mervyn Peake.

O here it is! and there it is!
And no-one knows whose share it is!
Nor dares to stake a claim —
But we have seen it in the air,
A fairy, like a William pear —
With but itself to blame.

A thug it is! and smug it is;
And like a floating pug it is,
Above the orchard trees.
It has no right — no right at all
To soar above the orchard wall
With chilblains on its knees.

I Have My Price

I have my price — it's rather high
(about the level of your eye)
but if you're nice to me I'll try
to lower it for you —

To lower it! To lower it!
Upon the kind of rope they knit
from yellow grass in Paraguay
where knitting is taboo.

Some knit them purl, some knit them plain
some knit their brows of pearl in vain.
Some are so plain, they try again
to tease the wool of love!
O felony in Paraguay
there's not a soul in Paraguay
who's worth the dreaming of.
They say,
who's worth the dreaming of.

I Waxes, and I Wanes, Sir

I waxes, and I wanes, sir;
    I ebbs's and I flows;
Some says it be my Brains, sir,
    Some says it be my Nose.

It isn't as I'm slow, sir,
    (To cut a story long),
It's just I'd LOVE to know, sir,
    Which one of them is WRONG.

John Phoenix (George H. Derby) (1824–61)

PHŒNIX'S PICTORIAL,

And Second Story Front Room Companion.

| Vol. I.] | San Diego, October 1, 1853. | [No. |

Portrait of His Royal Highness Prince Albert.—Prince Albert, th son of a gentleman named Coburg, is the husband of Queen Victori of England, and the father of many of her children. He is the invento of the celebrated "Albert hat," which has been lately introduced witl great effect in the U.S. Army. The Prince is of German extraction, hi father being a Dutchman and his mother a Duchess.

Mansion of John Phœnix, Esq., San Diego, California.

House in which Shakespeare was born, in Stratford-on-Avon.

Abbotsford, the residence of Sir Walter Scott, author of Byron's
Pilgrim's Progress, etc.

The Capitol at Washington.

Residence of Governor Bigler, at Benicia, California.

Battle of Lake Erie (*see remarks*. p. 96).

[96]

The Battle of Lake Erie, of which our Artist presents a spirited engraving, copied from the original painting, by Hannibal Carracci, in the possession of J. P. Haven, Esq., was fought in 1836, on Chesapeake Bay, between the U. S. frigates Constitution and Guerriere and the British troops under General Putnam. Our glorious flag, there as everywhere, was victorious, and "Long may it wave, o'er the land of the free and the home of *the slave*."

Fearful accident on the Camden & Amboy Railroad ! ! Terrible loss of life ! ! !

View of the City of San Diego, by Sir Benjamin West.

Interview between Mrs Harriet Beecher Stowe and the Duchess of Sutherland, from a group of Statuary, by Clarke Mills.

Shell of an Oyster once eaten by General Washington, showing the General's manner of opening Oysters.

There!—this is but a specimen of what we can do, if liberally sustained. We wait with anxiety to hear the verdict of the Public before proceeding to any farther and greater outlays.

Subscription, $5 per annum, payable invariably in advance.

INDUCEMENTS FOR CLUBBING.

Twenty copies furnished for one year, for fifty cents. Address John Phœnix, office of the *San Diego Herald*.

Sylvia Plath (1932–63)
Metaphors

I'm a riddle in nine syllables,
An elephant, a ponderous house,
A melon strolling on two tendrils.
O red fruit, ivory, fine timbers!
This loaf's big with its yeasty rising.
Money's new-minted in this fat purse.
I'm a means, a stage, a cow in calf.
I've eaten a bag of green apples,
Boarded the train there's no getting off.

Roger Price (1921–   )
Droodles

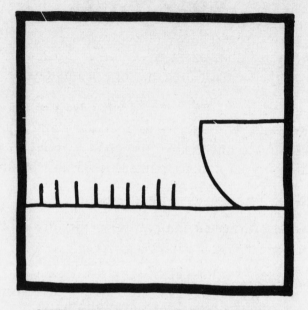

SHIP DESERTING SINKING RATS

PICCOLO PLAYER AS SEEN FROM INSIDE PICCOLO

Alexander Resnikoff (1894–)

Two Witches

There was a witch
The witch had an itch
The itch was so itchy it
Gave her a twitch.

Another witch
Admired the twitch
So she started twitching
Though she had no itch.

Now both of them twitch
So it's hard to tell which
Witch has the itch and
Which witch has the twitch.

Moss Rich (1920–)

Instructions for using your Japanese Pocket Calculator

(Based on the Instructions for using your
Japanese Pocket Calculator)

Take honble Thing and press her twice
If come to clear she very mice.
Then press twice one and make pluss two
Will show display at greening view.
To make chain calc. without swett blood
Follow instruct. as clear as mud.
At first make proint then minuss 9
If good result is very fine,
Pluss multiply dividing twice
Will give percentium of last price.
If figure shake and not too clear
She want new battery in rear.

If not result she make is sound
Then swing the lady round and round,
Thru' open window chuck away

And buy a new Thing same this day.
Go look in shop where all displayed —
Is very excellent for trade.

Follow the clear operating instructions carefully and
your appliance will give you many years of lifelong service

Robert Robinson (1927–   )
Doggerel

I met a Bishop in the street
With flat, ecclesiastic feet:
'Aha,' he said, 'another sinner —
Pray join me in a little dinner
To celebrate — please don't be shocked —
The fact that I have been unfrocked:
Last Thursday week at half past three
At Tunbridge Wells, by church decree,
For strolling in a drunken manner
Down Piccadilly with a banner
On which were hung, in taste devout,
My gaiters, and a quart of stout.
And now for food: most frequently
I feed on grass and warm beef-tea.
But sometimes — just a whim, my dear —
On buttered prunes and nettle beer.
'And speaking of hammer-toes,' he said,
'How far is it to Birkenhead?'
'Alas,' said I, 'I cannot swim,'
And sadly took my leave of him.
I wonder shall I ever meet
Another Bishop with flat feet?

Christina Rossetti (1830–94)

Fishy Tale

When fishes set umbrellas up
  If the rain-drops run,
Lizards will want their parasols
  To shade them from the sun.

The peacock has a score of eyes,
  With which he cannot see;
The cod-fish has a silent sound,
  However that may be.

No dandelions tell the time,
  Although they turn to clocks,
Cat's cradle does not hold the cat,
  Nor foxglove fit the fox.

W. C. Sellar (? –1951) and R. J. Yeatman (? –1968)

From 1066 And All That

Illustrated by John Reynolds and John Leech

Caesar Invades Britain

The first date[1] in English History is 55 BC in which year Julius Caesar (the *memorable* Roman Emperor) landed, like all other successful invaders of these islands, at Thanet. This was in the Olden Days, when the Romans were top nation on account of their classical education, etc.

Julius Caesar advanced very energetically, throwing his cavalry several thousands of paces over the River Flumen; but the Ancient Britons, though all well over military age, painted themselves true blue, or *woad*, and fought as heroically under their dashing queen, Woadicea, as they did later in thin red lines under their good queen Victoria.

Julius Caesar was therefore compelled to invade Britain again the following year (54 BC, not 56, owing to the peculiar Roman method of counting), and having defeated the Ancient Britons by unfair means,

[1] For the other date see 'William the Conqueror'

such as battering-rams, tortoises, hippocausts, centipedes, axes and bundles, set the memorable Latin sentence, 'Veni, Vidi, Vici,' which the Romans, who were all very well educated, construed correctly.

The Britons, however, who of course still used the old pronunciation, understanding him to have called them 'Weeny, Weedy and Weaky,' lost heart and gave up the struggle, thinking that he had already divided them All into Three Parts.

John, an Awful King

When John came to the throne he lost his temper and flung himself on the floor, foaming at the mouth and biting the rushes. He was thus a Bad King. Indeed, he had begun badly as a Bad Prince, having attempted to answer the Irish Question[1] by pulling the beards of the aged Irish chiefs, which was a Bad Thing and the wrong answer.

[1]N.B. The Irish Question at this time consisted of:
1. Some Norman Barons, who lived in a Pail (near Dublin).
2. The natives and Irish Chieftains, who were beyond the Pail, living in bogs, beards, etc.

Test Paper III

1. Contract, Expand, and Explode
   (a) The Charters and Garters of the Realm.
   (b) The Old Suspender.

2. How did any *one* of the following differ from any one of the other?
   (1) Henry IV, Part I.
   (2) Henry IV, Part II.

3. 'The end of the closing of the 2nd stage of the Treaty of Bretigny marks the opening of a new phase in the 1st stage of the termination of the Hundred Years War.' (Confute.)

4. 'Know ye not Agincourt?' (Confess.)

5. 'Uneasy lies the head that wears a Throne.'
   (a) Suggest remedies, or
   (b) Imitate the action of a Tiger.

6. Intone interminably (but inaudibly)
   i. The Pilgrims' Grace.
   ii. 'Cuccu.'

7. Do not draw a skotch-map of the Battle of Bannockburn but write not more than three lines on the advantages and disadvantages of the inductive historical method with special relation to ecclesiastical litigation in the earlier Lancastrian epochs.

8. How would you confuse
   (1) The Wars of the Roses?
   (2) Lamnel Simkin and Percy Warmneck?
   (3) The Royal issue?

9. Why do you picture John of Gaunt as a rather emaciated grandee?

10. Describe in excessive detail
    (a) The advantages of the Black Death.
    (b) The fate of the Duke of Clarence.
    (c) A Surfeit.

    N.B. — Candidates should write on at least one side of the paper.

Rufus. A Ruddy King

This monarch was always very angry and red in the face and was therefore unpopular, so that his death was a Good Thing: it occurred in the following memorable way. Rufus was hunting one day in the New Forest, when William Tell (the memorable crackshot, inventor of Crossbow puzzles) took unerring aim at a reddish apple, which had fallen on to the King's head, and shot him through the heart. Sir Isaac Walton, who happened to be present at the time, thereupon invented the Law of Gravity. Thus was the reign of Rufus brought to a Good End.

A Good Thing

Williamanmary for some reason was known as The Orange in their own country of Holland, and were popular as King of England because the people naturally believed it was decended from Nell Glyn. It was on the whole a good King and one of their first Acts was the Toleration Act, which said they would tolerate anything, though afterwards it went back on this and decided that they could not tolerate the Scots.

The Answer

Robert Service (1874–1958)

The Bread-Knife Ballad

I

A little child was sitting
Upon her mother's knee,
And down her cheeks the bitter tears did flow;
And as I sadly listened
I heard this tender plea;
'Twas uttered in a voice so soft and low:–

Chorus
Please, Mother, don't stab Father with the
    bread-knife,
Remember 'twas a gift when you were wed,
But if you *must* stab Father with the bread-knife,
Please, Mother, use another for the bread.

II

'Not guilty!' said the Jury,
And the Judge said: 'Set her free;
But remember, it must not occur again;
And next time you must listen
To you little daughter's plea.'
Then all the Court did join in this refrain:—

Chorus . . .

William Shakespeare (1564–1616)

From Love's Labour's Lost

ACT III

Sc. I. — The KING OF NAVARRE's Park
(Enter ARMADO and MOTH)

ARM: Warble, child; make passionate my sense of hearing.
MOTH: (*singing*) Concolinel,—
ARM: Sweet air! Go, tenderness of years; take this key, give enlargement to the swain, bring him festinately hither; I must
employ him in a letter to my love.
MOTH: Master, will you win your love with a French brawl?
ARM: How meanest thou? brawling in French?
MOTH: No, my complete master; but to jig off a tune at the tongue's
end, canary to it with your feet, humour it with turning up
your eyelids, sigh a note and sing a note, sometime through
the throat, as if you swallowed love by singing love, sometime through the nose, as if you snuffed up love by smelling
love; with your hat penthouse-like o'er the shop of your eyes;
with your arms crossed on your thin belly-doublet like a
rabbit on a spit; or your hands in your pocket like a man after
the old painting; and keep not too long in one tune, but a snip
and away. These are complements, these are humours, these
betray nice wenches, that would be betrayed without these;
and make them men of note, — do you note me? — that most
are affected to these.
ARM: How hast thou purchased this experience?
MOTH: By my penny of observation.

ARM: But O — but O, —

MOTH: 'The hobby-horse is forgot.'

ARM: Callest thou my love 'hobby-horse'?

MOTH: No, master; the hobby-horse is but a colt, and your love perhaps, a hackney. But have you forgot your love?

ARM: Almost I had.

MOTH: Negligent student! learn her by heart.

ARM: By heart, and in heart, boy.

MOTH: And out of heart, master: all those three I will prove:

ARM: What wilt thou prove?

MOTH A man, if I live; and this, by, in and without, upon the instant; by heart you love her, because your heart cannot come by her; in heart you love her, because your heart is in love with her; and out of heart you love her, being out of heart that you cannot enjoy her.

ARM: I am all these three.

MOTH: And three times as much more, and yet nothing at all.

ARM: Fetch hither the swain: he must carry me a letter.

MOTH: A message well sympathized: a horse to be ambassador for an ass.

ARM: Ha, ha! what sayest thou?

MOTH: Marry, sir, you must send the ass upon the horse, for he is very slow-gaited. But I go.

ARM: The way is but short; away!

MOTH: As swift as lead, sir.

ARM: Thy meaning, pretty ingenious? Is not lead a metal heavy, dull, and slow?

MOTH: *Minime*, honest master; or rather, master, no.

ARM: I say, lead is slow.

MOTH: You are too swift, sir, to say so: is that lead slow which is fir'd from a gun?

ARM: Sweet smoke of rhetoric! He reputes me a cannon; and the bullet, that's he:
I shoot thee at the swain.

MOTH: Thump then, and I flee. (*Exit*)

ARM: A most acute juvenal; volable and free of grace!
By thy favour, sweek welkin, I must sigh in thy face;
Most rude melancholy, valour gives thee place.
My heald is return'd.

(*Re-enter MOTH with COSTARD*)

MOTH: A wonder, master! here's a costard broken in a shin.

ARM: Some enigma, some riddle: come, thy *l'envoy*; begin.

COST: No egma, no riddle, no *l'envoy*; no salve in the mail, sir. O!
     sir, plantain, a plain plantain; no *l'envoy*, no *l'envoy*: no salve,
     sir, but a plantain.

ARM: By virtue, thou enforcest laughter; thy silly thought, my
     spleen; the heaving of my lungs provokes me to ridiculous
     smiling: O! pardon me, my stars. Doth the inconsiderate take
     salve for *l'envoy*, and the word *l'envoy* for a salve?

MOTH: Do the wise think them other? is not *l'envoy* a salve?

ARM: No, page: it is an epilogue or discourse, to make plain
     Some obscure precedence that hath tofore been sain.
     I will example it:
       The fox, the ape, and the humble-bee,
       Were still at odds, being but three.
     There's the moral. Now the *l'envoy*.

MOTH: I will add the *l'envoy*. Say the moral again.

ARM: The fox, the ape, and the humble-bee,
       Were still at odds, being but three.

MOTH: Until the goose came out of door,
       And stay'd the odds by adding four.
     Now will I begin your moral, and do you follow with my
     l'envoy.
       The fox, the ape, and the humble-bee,
       Were still at odds, being but three.

ARM: Until the goose came out of door,
       Staying the odds by adding four.

MOTH: A good *l'envoy*, ending in the goose. Would you desire more?

COST: The boy hath sold him a bargain, a goose, that's flat.
     Sir, your pennyworth is good an your goose be fat.
     To sell a bargain well is as cunning as fast and loose;
     Let me see; a fat *l'envoy*; ay, that's a fat goose.

ARM: Come hither, come hither. How did this argument begin?

MOTH: By saying that a costard was broken in a shin. Then call'd you
     for the *l'envoy*.

COST: True, and I for a plantain: thus came your argument in;
     Then the boy's fat *l'envoy*, the goose that you bought;
     And he ended the market.

ARM: But tell me; how was there a costard broken in a shin?

MOTH: I will tell you sensibly.

COST: Thou hast no feeling of it, Moth: I will speak that *l'envoy*;
     I, Costard, running out, that was safely within,
     Fell over the threshold and broke my shin.

ARM: We will talk no more of this matter.

From The Winter's Tale

ACT IV

Scene II
(Enter AUTOLYCUS, singing)

When daffodils begin to peer,
    With heigh! the doxy, over the dale,
Why, then comes in the sweet o' the year;
    For the red blood reigns in the winter's pale.

The white sheet bleaching on the hedge,
    With heigh! the sweet birds, O, how they sing!
Doth set my pugging tooth on edge;
    For a quart of ale is a dish for a king.

The lark, that tirra-lirra chants,
    With heigh! with heigh! the thrush and the jay.
Are summer songs for me and my aunts,
    While we lie tumbling in the hay.

Timothy Shy (D. B. Wyndham Lewis) (1894–1969)

Variations on a Simple Theme

The question is often asked in the Athenaeum Club 'How would Le Queux do?'; 'What would Ethel do with such and such a situation?' And a mellow episcopal voice may often add 'In what manner would Nat Gould treat it?' For Literature is justly honoured in that solemn place, where even Cabinet Ministers (Conservative) may be seen on hot summer afternoons swatting flies with the Times Literary Supplement. The event of the year, I am informed, was the Hodger Prize Competition for an imaginative work founded on a theme suggested by a member of the Literary Circle. The theme selected was a well-known verse of English lyric poetry.

Jack and Jill went up the hill
To get a pail of water;
Jack fell down and broke his crown
And Jill came tumbling after.

We may as well reprint characteristic extracts from the winning compositions.

The Stork's Nest

A complete short story from the Slavo-Jazcslovak of Bunga Piffzl

On the fourth floor of the old house in the suburbs of Jazzcsyl lived Jýl, a plump young woman with black sparkling eyes, with her aged parents. Jýl was always laughing, and when her old father stamped screaming on her mother's wrinkled, careworn face she would smile and say, 'How beautiful is the Spring! How lovely the elder-blossom! How white the snow on Hjycszlcsy!' On the floor below lived the young workman Ják, a tall handsome youth whose father had been a convict but was now caretaker of the town museum. When he met Jýl on the stairs Ják would say, 'How I love your little young fat face! It is as lovely as a round new white soft Grnórkscy cheese!'; and Jýl would laugh, and Ják would laugh too and finger his knife under his blouse, for he loved her. In the old house Jýl's mother lay under the bed and never stopped screaming, the pigs and hens ran about the place grunting and chirping with pleasure, and Jýl would laugh and sing 'How beautiful is the elder-tree!' All was sunshine in the old house; even the lean dark peasant in the basement flogged his thin weak wife with a happy smile, and the married couple from Sznórcz often stopped biting each other to sing about the Spring and the willows. Every time Ják met Jýl on the Stairs he would say, 'How perfect is your young white large neck!' and he longed to plunge his knife into the girl. How the sun shone! And the little white clouds sailed over the roof-tops and over the lime-trees! Jýl would laugh at them, and Ják would laugh too, and stab at anyone who happened to be passing, out of pure happiness.

One day, Ják, meeting the girl on the stairs, said 'How I love your thin small straight feet! Let us go up the hill! How I hate the nose of my aunt! It is like an old thick red hat. How beautiful the wind is on the hill, and the lilac is out. I must go a draw water for the old women. Grzcsh!' And Jýl said with a merry laugh, 'Yes, we will go together! The buds are out on the plane-trees. Hurrah for the Spring!' and hand in hand they wandered out of the suburbs, past the market-gardens of Ksńmsc, out into the wide country, and up the hill to the spring, where Ják drew a bucket of the cold clear water and fell to the ground, bruising his head, with Jýl sliding and falling beside him; but all she said was 'Hark at the birds in the elder-trees! Hurrah!' She tied up Ják's wound with a shawl her aunt Tázsca had brought from the fair of Pólcszovny and they returned home. As they passed the corner of the street where they lived they heard the old house resounding with yells, and Jýl laughed and said to Ják, 'Hark! They are happy! It is the Spring!' and ran indoors, but Ják took a very large knife from his blouse and stuck it into a very old man who was standing near and screaming, and when Jýl came laughing down the stairs he said gaily, 'Look, Jýl! He has an old hairy face like a little piece of mud!' and as the girl stopped to look he raised his knife again.

'How they all bleed,' thought Ják, suddenly despondent, listening to the howls of the old women in the house.

From *The Secret Hill*

Note: This manuscript novel bore no signature, and appears to be the joint work of two or three serious analytical novelists. It is a most unhealthy tale, and full of repressions and introspective morbidity. It is not clear whether it is of English or American origin, but is the sort of thing that would get a column in the heavier reviews.

In the first fourteen chapters the heroine is struggling with something which may be either the Medea-complex or an ingrowing toe-nail; it is not quite clear which. Anyway it is very unhealthy. We will quote an extract from the scene where she has a nerve-storm about something on the farm, but it is all curiously muffled and significant, like a neurotic woman with large teeth speaking through five layers of blanket, and of course very brilliant.

XV

He came to her in the afternoon and said abruptly, 'I am going to the hill.'

'The hill?'

'Yes.'

She felt the dark waters rushing over her again, rushing from him to her. She heard him speaking, as it were, from within herself, from an infinite distance, and yet near, and within herself another voice was repeating drearily, 'The hill. The hill. The hill. The hill. The hill.' She felt as though the moment had come at last when her inmost soul shuddered and recoiled, with a dreary knowledge of what was between her and him—and yet not between, but as it were something

outside herself, something she could not see, definite and precise yet
looming ever nearer and away, so that she felt herself saying, 'No, No,'
and then, 'But yes, Yes,' and grappling dimly (so it seemed to her) with
the tremendous urging of necessity; and so she straightened herself to
receive, as it were, what might be coming, conscious — or unconscious? she could not have said — that from him to her, inevitably,
almost, there passed half-felt, half-feared, wholly incomprehensible
floods of beingness, great searching tides that washed in and out of
her and left her feeling — what? She did not yet know.

He was speaking again, more sharply.

'I am going for water. I shall take the bucket.'

'The bucket?'

'Yes.'

She caught her breath sharply. So this, then, was what she had
been half-visualising, half-fleeing from, half catching to her breast in
the hope that he would, somehow, have given her of his own will
something she could not formulate even to herself, save that she felt it
to be, reaching out and grasping and retiring again, and, as it were,
clutching at her consciousness — for so she deemed it — and fading
again into a kind of interior dullness of experience which made her
ache, though she said to herself, 'No, No'; but then again the reassur-
ing return of that previous half-glimpsed permanence, the half-dim
hope, as she realised it, spreading out and broadening from her to
him, and narrowing and becoming more implied and constant, and
concentrating finally in a crystallised and palpable imminence. . .

'What is that paper you are tearing up?' he asked, sharply.

She looked down. It was a page of *The Delphic*. Strange, she
thought dully, that it should be that! It was her favourite magazine.
She found in it the vague echo of her own thoughts, and often, when
striving to formulate, to impel, some enveloping idea that wrapped
her round oozily like warm, wet cotton-wool she had thought of
writing it down — if indeed she could tear it from herself and rid
herself of its soft, clinging, amorphous embrace — and sending it to
the Editor in place of his own leading article.

'Will you come?' he said, more kindly, glimpsing the tremendous
forces at war in her. 'I am going to take the old yellow wooden
bucket.'

Old? Yellow? Wooden? She tried to quiet her storming nerves, to
grasp the significance of what he was saying.

'Why?'

'To get water.'

She shrank back, trying to hold off, as it were, to repel, to push
away, to drive out, expel the hidden consciousness that rose like a

wall between her and the realisation she felt surging beneath her, the
purpose of her hidden aspiring, the panting urgency of the current
that, so it seemed to her, pulsated and swung out and poured back
and flooded her with an unformulated dread of understating —
perhaps overemphasising, perhaps sidetracking — the accumulated
force of static inhibitions which bound her thought — how loosely,
how incoherently, with what secret value she knew not — to his.

'You are going to the hill?' Her voice was quite flat and toneless
now.

'Yes.'

'To get water?'

'Yes. In the bucket.'

'Where from?'

She held her breath. The answer came slowly.

'The well.'

She heard herself repeating dully under her breath.

'The well. The well. The well. The well. The well. The well.'

'Will you come?' His voice had a pleading urgent note.

'Where?'

'To the hill.'

'What is there?'

'The well. I am going to get water.' (Water!)

He said very slowly and distinctly, 'I shall take the bucket.' (The
bucket!)

'Now?'

'Yes.'

'Why?'

'To get water.'

She checked herself in the very act of saying 'what in?' She did not
know what made her stop saying that. But rather wearily, and with a
defeated sense that there were hesitancies at work in her soul, trying
to encompass, to envelop, to surround, to conquer, to inhabit the
fastness of her comprehension, she rose and went upstairs to put on
her hat.

Peter Simple (Michael Wharton) (1913–   )

'Pop Notes' by Jim Droolberg

The Filthy Swine, with their folk hit 'My Girl's Head Comes to a Point'
again head the Top Twenty this week. The Bedbugs' 'Chewing Old

Socks With You' goes down to third place and Cliff Alopecea moves up with 'Individual Fruit Pie of Love'.

Wanda Drainstorm's 'My Old Plastic Granny' stays steady at number four and the Cockroaches have rocketed up from eleventh to fifth place with 'Love Crawled Under the Door'.

The Drips, whose 'Softening of the Brain' kept fifth place for three weeks running, suddenly collapsed and fell out of the charts altogether. Their manager has had them destroyed.

Realism

When Piledriver Films took over the pretty village of Dorminster Monachorum, in Dorset, to make a new horror film, 'Wittgenstein and the Curse of the Pharaohs', they made certain changes in the place.

A stream which flowed through the village was dammed to form a small lake, which at once engulfed several cottages. The village pub was partly demolished to make it more like the ruined inn in Transylvania called for in the script.

The church was equipped with a new tower where croaking ravens could be better accommodated. The rectory was burned down and replaced by a capacious pyramid, and a bat-haunted gloomy, pine-wood, convenient for lurking ghouls and vampires, was planted in the garden.

Brian Hohenzollern, the director, had undertaken to put everything back as it was before as soon as shooting was completed. But there was a certain amount of resentment among the locals all the same.

During the filming of a scene where the eccentric, banana-guzzling Cambridge philosopher, played by Bruce Braganza, was chased down the village street by an Ancient Egyptian mummy (Stan Bourbon Parma) and a sinister blonde girl archaeologist (Kay Wittelsbach) and in self-defence exploded a small atomic bomb, things came to a head.

An angry mob of villagers, brandishing pitchforks, cudgels, bicycle-pumps, horse-brasses and warming-pans, tried to rush the cameras. But Hohenzollern, resourceful as ever, ordered machine-guns to be turned on them, and the scene was incorporated in the spectacular combined orgy, massacre, holocaust, deluge and outbreak of bubonic plague which forms the climax of the film.

N. F. Simpson (1919–   )

From At Least It's a Precaution against Fire

(MIDDIE to door. She opens it. COUNCIL OFFICIAL)

OFFICIAL:	Good morning. Mrs Paradock? I'm the Inspector of W... and Legacies. I gather you have reason to think you r... the victim of an unauthorised bequest.
MIDDIE:	That's right. You've come from next door, haven't yo...

(OFFICIAL comes in and they go to the kitchen)

OFFICIAL:	Yes, I've just been in there looking at an old brass bedstead.

(Kitchen. MIDDIE with OFFICIAL to BRO.)

MIDDIE:	This is the Inspector of Wills and Legacies. He's come to look at the. . .

(OFFICIAL makes straight for it and gives it a professional once-over)

BRO:	We wondered if it might be. . .
OFFICIAL:	. . . an unauthorised bequest. Yes. Let's have a thorough dekko.

(He takes out a watchmaker's eyeglass, puts it in his eye and has a close look)

OFFICIAL:	Yes. Not much doubt that it's a fire extinguisher, anyhow. You can tell by the . . . *(He outlines the shape with his hands)* and the fact that it's in a glass case for ease of access.
MIDDIE:	What we were rather wondering was how it got there.
OFFICIAL:	Oh — that's the least of our worries, frankly. They get in anywhere they can. Open window, door left unlocked. Easiest thing in the world. Dump it down on the table and scarper.
BRO:	You mean there's a gang at work?
OFFICIAL:	Could be a gang. Could be somebody working on his own.
MIDDIE:	But why us?

OFFICIAL:	It's like lightning, Mrs Paradock. It could strike any-where. On the other hand it could be somebody with a grudge. Somebody with a grudge and an attic-full of old junk. That's the likeliest explanation.
BRO:	I can't imagine who that could be.
MIDDIE:	The only person I can think of with an attic-full of old junk is little old Mrs Cobley-Willet.
BRO:	Yes, but it's not her, Middie.
OFFICIAL:	(*Making note*) Little old Mrs Who?
MIDDIE:	Mrs Cobley-Willet. She lives a door or two along.
BRO:	Middie. Can you really see Mrs Cobley-Willet. . . (*to Official*) She's ninety-three.
OFFICIAL:	We'll have a word with her. They sometimes get some strange ideas at that age. You'd be surprised. Had trouble with her before, have you?
BRO:	Not to say trouble — have we?
MIDDIE:	I wouldn't put anything past her.
OFFICIAL:	It doesn't really sound like an old lady of ninety-three. We generally find they like to hold on to their old junk, but you never know.
BRO:	I suppose once you've identified who it is, they can be made to come and take possession of it again.
OFFICIAL:	Ah, well, now — that's where our hands are a bit tied, you see, as I was saying to the lady next door with regard to the bedstead. This is a carefully thought out job. Somebody with legal training.
BRO:	You mean we can never get rid of it?
OFFICIAL:	I wouldn't go as far as to say you could never get rid of it, but what you've got hold of here, you see, is what we class as an heirloom.
BRO:	It's been handed down, in other words.
OFFICIAL:	Exactly.
MIDDIE:	You mean from generation to generation?
OFFICIAL:	Oh yes. Quite some way back judging by the overall appearance of it. Probably part originally of a collection of pickled walnuts belonging to the Earl of Walthamstow, or something of that kind — unless it's a forgery.
MIDDIE:	If it belongs to the Earl of Walthamstow, what's it doing here?
OFFICIAL:	Any one of a number of possibilities, Mrs Paradock.

	A lot of these old pieces went astray during the war. It could be one of those.
BRO:	Looted, you mean?
OFFICIAL:	No, I shouldn't think so. More likely bequeathed to somebody in the blackout, and went to the wrong person by mistake. Easily happen. The trouble is — once they've been handed down, they're the devil's own job to hand back up again.
BRO:	But it hasn't been handed down to us. It was on the table when we came in.
OFFICIAL:	I'm afraid you're living in a fool's paradise, Mr Paradock. This is a legacy.
MIDDIE:	You mean someone's waited till our back was turned. . .?
OFFICIAL:	. . . and made you the beneficiaries under a will.
BRO:	But that's . . .

John Skelton (1460–1529)

Mannerly Margery Milk and Ale

Ay, beshrew you! by my fay,
These wanton clerks be nice alway!
Avaunt, avaunt, my popinjay!
What, will ye do nothing but play?
Tilly vally, straw, let be I say!
Gup, Christian Clout, gup, Jack of the Vale!
With Mannerly Margery Milk and Ale.

By God, ye be a pretty pode,
And I love you an whole cart-load.
Straw, James Foder, ye play the fode,
I am no hackney for your rod:
Go watch a bull, your back is broad!
Gup, Christian Clout, gup, Jack of the Vale!
With Mannerly Margery Milk and Ale.

Ywis ye deal uncourteously;
What, would ye frumple me? now fy!
What, and ye shall be my pigesnye?
By Christ, ye shall not, no hardely:

I will not be japèd bodily!
Gup, Christian Clout, gup, Jack of the Vale!
With Mannerly Margery Milk and Ale.

Walk forth your way, ye cost me nought;
Now have I found that I have sought:
The best cheap flesh that ever I bought.
Yet, for His love that all that wrought,
Wed me, or else I die for thought.
Gup, Christian Clout, your breath is stale!
Go, Mannerly Margery Milk and Ale!
Gup, Christian Clout, gup, Jack of the Vale!
With Mannerly Margery Milk and Ale.

To Mistress Margaret Hussey

 Merry Margaret
 As Midsummer flower,
 Gentle as falcon
 Or hawk of the tower:
With solace and gladness,
Much mirth and no madness,
All good and no badness;
 So joyously
 So maidenly,
 So womanly
 Her demeaning
 In every thing,
 Far, far passing
 That I can indite,
 Or suffice to write
Of Merry Margaret
As midsummer flower
Gentle as falcon
Or hawk of the tower.
As patient and still
And as full of good will
As fair Isaphill,
Coliander,
Sweet pomander,
Good Cassander;

Steadfast of thought,
Well made, well wrought,
Far may be sought,
Ere that ye can find
So courteous, so kind
As merry Margaret,
This midsummer flower,
Gentle as falcon
Or hawk of the tower.

Stevie Smith (1903–71)

Tenuous and Precarious

Tenuous and Precarious
Were my guardians,
Precarious and Tenuous,
Two Romans.

My father was Hazardous,
Hazardous,
Dear old man,
Three Romans.

There was my brother Spurious,
Spurious Posthumous,
Spurious was spurious
Was four Romans.

My husband was Perfidious,
He was perfidious,
Five Romans.

Surreptitious, our son,
Was surreptitious,
He was six Romans.

Our cat Tedious
Still lives,
Count not Tedious
Yet.

My name is Finis,
Finis, Finis,
I am Finis,
Six, five, four, three, two,
One Roman,
Finis.

The Grange

Oh there hasn't been much change
At The Grange.

Of course the blackberries growing closer
Make getting in a bit of a poser
But there hasn't been much change
At The Grange.

Old Sir Prior died
They say on the point of leaving for the seaside
They never found the body which seemed odd to some
(Not me, seeing as what I seen the butler done)

Oh there hasn't been much change
At The Grange.

The governess as got it now
Miss Ursy having moved down to The Green Cow
Seems proper done out of er rights a b. shame
And what's that the governess pushes round at
    nights in the old pram?

No there hasn't been much change
At The Grange.

The shops leave their stuff at the gates now —
    meat, groceries
Mostly old canned goods you know from McInnes's
They wouldn't go up to the door,
Not after what happened to Fred's pa.

Oh there hasn't been much change
At The Grange.

Parsing there early this morning, cor lummy,
I hears a whistling sound coming from the old chimney
Whistling it was fit to bust and not a note wrong
The old pot, whistling the *Death of Nelson*.

Oh there hasn't been much change
At The Grange.

But few goes that way somehow
Not now.

Jonathan Swift (1667–1745)

Verses Made for Women Who Cry Apples, &c.

Apples

Come buy my fine Wares,
Plumbs, Apples and Pears,
A hundred a Penny,
In Conscience too many,
Come, will you have any;
My Children are seven,
I wish them in Heaven,
My Husband's a Sot,
With his Pipe and his Pot,
Not a Farthing will gain 'em,
And I must maintain 'em.

Asparagus

Ripe 'Sparagrass,
Fit for Lad or Lass,
To make their Water pass:
O, 'tis pretty Picking
With a tender Chicken.

Onyons

Come, follow me by the Smell,
Here's delicat Onyons to sell,
I promise to use you well.
They make the Blood warmer,
You'll feed like a Farmer:
For this is ev'ry Cook's Opinion,
No sav'ry Dish without an Onyon:
But lest your Kissing should be spoyl'd,
Your Onyons must be th'roughly boyl'd;
  Or else you may spare
  Your Mistress a Share,
The Secret will never be known;
  She cannot discover
  The Breath of her Lover,
But think it as sweet as her own.

Oysters

Charming Oysters I cry,
My Masters come buy,
So plump and so fresh,
So sweet is their Flesh,
No *Colchester* Oyster,
Is sweeter and moyster,
Your Stomach they settle,
And rouse up your Mettle,
They'll make you a Dad
Of a Lass or a Lad;
And, Madam your Wife
They'll please to the Life;
Be she barren, be she old,
Be she Slut, or be she Scold,
Eat my Oysters, and lye near her,
She'll be fruitful, never fear her.

Herrings

Be not sparing,
Leave off swearing
Buy my Herring
Fresh from *Malahide*,
Better ne'er was try'd.
Come eat 'em with pure fresh Butter and Mustard,
Their Bellies are soft, and as white as a Custard.
Come, Six-pence a Dozen to get me some Bread,
Or, like my own Herrings, I soon shall be dead.

Oranges

Come, buy my fine Oranges, Sauce for your Veal,
And charming when squeez'd in a Pot of brown Ale.
Well roasted, with Sugar and Wine in a Cup,
They'll make a sweet Bishop when Gentlefolks sup.

William Makepeace Thackeray (1811–63)

A Tragic Story

There lived a sage in days of yore,
And he a handsome pigtail wore;
But wondered much and sorrowed more,
Because it hung behind him.

He mused upon this curious case,
And swore he'd change the pigtail's place
And have it hanging at his face,
Not dangling there behind him.

Says he, 'The Mystery I've found, —
I'll turn me round,'
He turned him round;
But still it hung behind him.

Then round and round, and out and in,
All day the puzzled sage did spin;

In vain — it mattered not a pin —
The pigtail hung behind him.

And right, and left, and round about,
And up and down, and in, and out
He turned; but still the pigtail stout
Hung steadily behind him.

And though his efforts never slack,
And though he twist, and twirl, and tack,
Alas! still faithful to his back,
The pigtail hangs behind him.

Dylan Thomas (1914—53)

From Holiday Memory

And the woman who lived next door came into the kitchen and said
that her mother, an ancient uncertain body who wore a hat with
cherries, was having 'one of her days' and had insisted, that very
holiday morning, in carrying all the way to the tram-stop a photograph album and the cut-glass fruit-bowl from the front room.

This was the morning when father, mending one hole in the thermos-
flask, made three; when the sun declared war on the butter, and the
butter ran; when dogs, with all the sweet-binned backyards to wag
and sniff and bicker in, chased their tails in the jostling kitchen,
worried sandshoes, snapped at flies, writhed between legs, scratched
among towels, sat smiling on hampers.

And if you could have listened at some of the open doors of some of
the houses in the street you might have heard:

'Uncle Owen says he can't find the bottle-opener. . .'
'Has he looked under the hallstand?'
'Willy's cut his finger. . .'
'Got your spade?'
'If somebody doesn't kill that dog. . .'
'Uncle Owen says why should the bottle-opener be under the hall-
stand?'
'Never again, never again. . .'
'I know I put the pepper somewhere. . .'

'Willy's bleeding. . .'
'Look, there's a bootlace in my bucket. . .'
'Oh come *on*, come on. . .'
'Let's have a look at the bootlace in your bucket. . .'
'If I lay my hands on that dog. . .'
'Uncle Owen's found the bottle-opener. . .'
'Willy's bleeding over the cheese. . .'

J. R. R. Tolkein (1892–1973)
The Man in the Moon Stayed up Too Late

There is an inn, a merry old inn
   beneath an old grey hill,
And there they brew a beer so brown
That the Man in the Moon himself came down
   one night to drink his fill.

The ostler has a tipsy cat
   that plays a five-stringed fiddle;
And up and down he runs his bow,
Now squeaking high, now purring low,
   now sawing in the middle.

The landlord keeps a little dog
   that is mighty fond of jokes;
When there's good cheer among the guests,
He cocks an ear at all the jests
   and laughs until he chokes.

They also keep a hornèd cow
   as proud as any queen;
But music turns her head like ale,
And makes her wave her tufted tail
   and dance upon the green.

And O! the row of silver dishes
   and the store of silver spoons!
For Sunday there's a special pair,
And these they polish up with care
   on Saturday afternoons.

The Man in the Moon was drinking deep,
   and the cat began to wail;
A dish and a spoon on the table danced,
The cow in the garden madly pranced,
   and the little dog chased his tail.

The Man in the Moon took another mug,
   and then rolled beneath his chair;
And there he dozed and dreamed of ale,
Till in the sky the stars were pale,
   and dawn was in the air.

The ostler said to his tipsy cat:
   'The white horses of the Moon,
They neigh and champ their silver bits;
But their master's been and drowned his wits,
   and the Sun'll be rising soon!'

So the cat on his fiddle played hey-diddle-didle,
   a jig that would wake the dead:
He squeaked and sawed and quickened the tune,
While the landlord shook the Man in the Moon:
   'It's after three!' he said.

They rolled the Man slowly up the hill
   and bundled him into the Moon,
While his horses galloped up in rear,
And the cow came capering like a deer,
   and a dish ran up with a spoon.

Now quicker the fiddle went deedle-dum-diddle;
   the dog began to roar,
The cow and the horses stood on their heads;
The guests all bounded from their beds
   and danced upon the floor.

With a ping and a pong the fiddle-strings broke!
   the cow jumped over the Moon,
And the little dog laughed to see such fun,
And the Saturday dish went off at a run
   with the silver Sunday spoon.

> The round Moon rolled behind the hill,
> as the Sun raised up her head.
> She hardly believed her fiery eyes;
> For though it was day, to her surprise
> they all went back to bed!

Mark Twain (Samuel Clemens) (1835–1910)

Our Italian Guide

In this connection I wish to say one word about Michael Angelo Buonarotti — I used to worship the mighty genius of Michael Angelo — that man who was great in poetry, painting, sculpture, architecture — great in everything he undertook. But I do not want Michael Angelo for breakfast — for luncheon — for dinner — for tea — for supper — for between meals. I like a change, occasionally. In Genoa, he designed everything; in Milan, he or his pupils designed everything; he designed the Lake of Como; in Padua, Verona, Venice, Bologna, who did we ever hear of, from guides, but Michael Angelo? In Florence, he painted everything, designed everything, nearly, and what he did not design he used to sit on a favourite stone and look at, and then they showed us the stone. In Pisa, he designed everything but the old shot-tower, and they would have attributed that to him if it had not been so awfully out of the perpendicular. He designed the piers of Leghorn and the custom-house regulations of Civita Vecchia. But here — here it is frightful. He designed St Peter's; he designed the Pope; he designed the Pantheon, the uniform of the Pope's soldiers; the Tiber, the Vatican, the Coliseum, the Capitol, the Tarpeian Rock, the Barberini Palace, St John Lateran, the Campagna, the Appian Way, the Seven Hills, the Baths of Caracalla, the Claudian Aqueduct, the Cloaca Maxima — the eternal bore designed the Eternal City, and unless all men and books do lie, he painted everything in it! Dan said the other day to the guide, 'Enough, enough, enough! Say no more! Lump the whole thing! say that the Creator made Italy from designs by Michael Angelo!'

I never felt so fervently thankful, so soothed, so tranquil, so filled with a blessed peace, as I did yesterday when I learned that Michael Angelo was dead.

But we have taken it out of this guide. He has marched us through miles of pictures and sculpture in the vast corridors of the Vatican; and through miles of pictures and sculpture in twenty other palaces;

he has shown us the great picture in the Sistine Chapel, and frescoes enough to fresco the heavens — pretty much all done by Michael Angelo. So with him we have played that game which has vanquished so many guides for us — imbecility and idiotic questions. These creatures never suspect — they have no idea of a sarcasm.

He shows us a figure and says: 'Statoo brunzo.' (Bronze statue).

We look at it indifferently, and the doctor asks: 'By Michael Angelo?'

'No — not know who.'

Then he shows us the ancient Roman Forum. The doctor asks: 'Michael Angelo?'

A stare from the guide. 'No — thousan' year before he is born.'

Then an Egyptian obelisk. Again: 'Michael Angelo?'

'Oh, *mon dieu*, genteelmen! Zis is *two* thousan' year before he is born!'

He grows so tired of that unceasing question, sometimes, that he dreads to show us anything at all. The wretch has tried all the ways he can think of to make us comprehend that Michael Angelo is only responsible for the creation of a *part* of the world, but somehow he has not succeeded yet. Relief for overtasked eyes and brain from study and sight-seeing is necessary, or we shall become idiotic sure enough. Therefore this guide must continue to suffer. If he does not enjoy it, so much the worse for him. We do.

In this place I may as well jot down a chapter concerning those necessary nuisances, European guides. Many a man has wished in his heart he could do without his guide; but knowing he could not, has wished he could get some amusement out of him as a remuneration for the affliction of his society. We accomplished this latter matter, and if our experience can be made useful to others, they are welcome to it.

The guides in Genoa are delighted to secure an American party, because Americans so much wonder, and deal so much in sentiment and emotion, before any relic of Columbus. Our guide there fidgeted about as if he had swallowed a spring mattress. He was full of animation — full of impatience. He said:

'Come wis me genteelmen! — come! I show you ze letter writing by Christopher Colombo! — write it himself! — write it wis his own hand! — come!'

He took us to the municipal palace. After much impressive fumbling of keys and opening of locks, the stained and aged document was spread before us. The guide's eyes sparkled. He danced about us and tapped the parchment with his finger:

'What I tell you, genteelmen! Is it not so? See! handwriting Christopher Colombo! — write it himself!'

We looked indifferent — unconcerned. The doctor examined the document very deliberately, during a painful pause. Then he said, without any show of interest:

'Ah — Ferguson — what — what did you say was the name of the party who wrote this?'

'Christopher Colombo! ze great Christopher Colombo!'

Another deliberate examination.

'Ah — did he write it himself, or — or how?'

'He write it himself! — Christopher Colombo! he's own hand-writing, write by himself!'

Then the doctor laid the document down and said:

'Why, I have seen boys in America only fourteen years old that could write better than that.'

'But zis is ze great Christo —'

'I don't care who it is! It's the worst writing I ever saw. Now you musn't think you can impose on us because we are strangers. We are not fools, by a good deal. If you have got any specimens of penmanship of real merit, trot them out! — and if you haven't, drive on!'

We drove on. The guide was considerably shaken up, but he made one more venture. He had something which he thought would overcome us. He said:

'Ah, genteelmen, you come wis me! I show you beautiful, O, magnificent bust Christopher Colombo! — splendid, grand, magnificent!'

He brought us before the beautiful bust — for it *was* beautiful — and sprang back and struck an attitude:

'Ah, look, genteelmen! — beautiful, grand — bust Christopher Colombo! — beautiful bust, beautiful pedestal!'

The doctor put up his eyeglass — procured for such occasions:

'Ah — what did you say this gentleman's name was?'

'Christopher Colombo! — ze great Christopher Colombo!'

'Christopher Colombo — the great Christopher Colombo. Well, what did *he* do?'

'Discover America! — discover America. Oh, ze devil!'

'Discover America! No — that statement will hardly wash. We are just from America ourselves. We heard nothing about it. Christopher Colombo — pleasant name — is — is he dead?'

'Oh, corpo di Baccho! — three hundred year!'

'What did he die of?

'I do not know! — I can not tell.'

'Small-pox, think?'

'I do not know, genteelmen! I do not know *what* he die of!'

'Measles, likely?'

'May be — may be — I do *not* know — I think he die of somethings.'

'Parents living?'

'Im-posseeble!'

'Ah — which is the bust and which is the pedestal?'

'Santa Maria! — *zis* ze bust! — *zis* ze pedestal!'

'Ah, I see, I see — happy combination — very happy combination, indeed. Is — is this the first time this gentleman was ever on a bust?'

That joke was lost on the foreigner — guides cannot master the subtleties of the American joke.

We have made it interesting for this Roman guide. Yesterday we spent three or four hours in the Vatican again, that wonderful world of curiosities. We came very near expressing interest, sometimes — even admiration — it was very hard to keep from it. We succeeded, though. Nobody else ever did, in the Vatican museums. The guide was bewildered — nonplussed. He walked his legs off, nearly, hunting up extraordinary things, and exhausted all his ingenuity on us, but it was a failure; we never showed any interest in anything. He had reserved what he considered to be his greatest wonder till the last — a royal Egyptian mummy, the best preserved in the world, perhaps. He took us there. He felt so sure, this time, that some of his old enthusiasm came back to him:

'See, genteelmen! — Mummy! Mummy!'

The eye-glass came up as calmly, as deliberately as ever.

'Ah — Ferguson — what did I understand you to say the gentleman's name was?'

'Name? — he got no name! — Mummy! — 'Gyptian mummy!'

'Yes, yes. Born here?'

'No! *'Gyptian* mummy!'

'Ah, just so. Frenchman, I presume?'

'No! — *not* Frenchman, not Roman! — born in Egypta!'

'Born in Egypta. Never heard of Egypta before. Foreign locality, likely. Mummy-mummy. How calm he is — how self-possessed. Is, ah — is he dead?'

'Oh, *sacre bleu*, been dead three thousan' year!'

The doctor turned on him savagely:

'Here, now, what do you mean by such conduct as this! Playing us for Chinamen because we are strangers, and trying to learn! Trying to impose your vile second-hand carcasses on *us!* — thunder and lightning, I've a notion to — to — if you've got a nice *fresh* corpse, fetch him out! — or, by George, we'll *brain* you!'

Stanley Unwin (1911–   )

On the Subject of TV and Radio Reception and Hearing the News in Dutch

Satellite is this fine, up shoot-F-t! scape velocity, right, twenty thou
sand milode macritical, very criticold position. A line of sight so tha
the televisuhold hup and straight downlode to your eyebold as you s
before the glass knothole in the front room there . . . Well, I listeny
news from Hilverso Holland. Would you like me to do a fundamoker
Well, this voice said (I listenode spessly news here) and he said 'Here
hellava dolloperlollander, hayrest unserer newserberichter innet
Nederfallops' — it means that in the dyke (coz hollows very clim
land, if you understand my meal, so far as Sarticulture) and the water
leakit and a very brave little Dutch man come and stuffy fingold in the
dykey-hole and stop the water driblit'n dribbly save the town get
floody-ho. So the reward'n Amsterdole with national honours and
statue like Handy Grimm. O joy with celebrakers with peopleode fla
on the bokus 'til the early maud!

John Updike (1932–   )
Superman

I drive my car to supermarket,
The way I take is superhigh,
A superlot is where I park it,
And Super Suds are what I buy.

Supersalesmen sell me tonic —
Super-Tone–O, for relief.
The planes I ride are supersonic.
In trains, I like the Super Chief.

Supercilious men and women
Call me superficial — me
Who so superbly learned to swim in
Supercolossality.

Superphosphate-fed foods feed me;
Superservice keeps me new.
Who would dare to supersede me,
Super-super-superwho?

J. J. Webster (1920–   )
La Forza del Destino (The Force of Destiny)

Now momma an' poppa they gotta ragazzo
So much-a he eat-a they call a-heem Fatso
He cry-a so loud-a they theenk eet-a propera
Some day he grow up-a an' seeng at L'opera,
Tenoré per'aps or a-basso profondo
For heem-a they spare-a no sforzo or fondo
An' cart a-heem off to La Scala Milano;
But Fatso he seeng like da clapped-out soprano,
La vocé don't flow, eet a-got no vibrato
Da notes a-come out-a all corsa an' flat-o
So momma an' poppa they coax an' cosseti
An' feed a-heem up with a-plenty spaghetti
An' always they press heem 'Bel-canto! Bel-canto!!'
When poor leedle Fatso he not-a a-wanto.
'Mangiaré an' train-a!' matino an' notte
Unteel a-da strain-a cet send a-heem potty,
Then momma an' poppa they cry een da vino
They not a-much like a-da forza destino,
An' down at L'opera il vocé supremo
He flog a-da programmes an' ice a-da cremo.

Reed Whittemore (1919—   )
The Party

They served tea in the sandpile, together with
Mudpies baked on the sidewalk.
After tea
The youngest said that he had had a good dinner,
The oldest dressed for a dance,
And they sallied forth together with watering pots
To moisten a rusted fire truck on account of it
Might rain.

I watched them from my study,
Thought of my part in these contributions to gaiety,
And resolved that the least acknowledgement I could make
Would be to join them;

                              so we
All took our watering pots (now filled with pies)
And poured tea on our dog. Then I kissed the children
And told them that when they grew up we would have
Real tea parties.
'That did be fun!' the oldest shouted, and ate pies
With wild surmise.

T. H. White (1906–64)

The Witch's Work Song

Two spoons of sherry
Three oz. of yeast,
Half a pound of unicorn,
And God bless the feast.
Shake them in the collander,
Bang them to a chop,
Simmer slightly, snip up nicely,
Jump, skip, hop.
Knit one, knot one, purl two together,
Pip one and pop one and pluck the secret feather.

Baste in a mod. oven,
God bless our coven.
Tra-la-la!
Three toads in a jar.
Te-he-he!
Put in the frog's knee,
Peep out of the lace curtain.
There goes the Toplady girl, she's up to no good
    that's certain.
Oh, what a lovely baby!
How nice it would go with gravy.
Pinch the salt,
Turn the malt
With a hey-nonny-nonny and I don't mean maybe.

Robb Wilton (1881–1957)

From Back Answers

A sail on the sea
Is a thing that suits me,
And I've done some sailing, it's true;
I've been at m' wits end
When sailing to Land's End
And one night — when I'd 'ad one or two —
The Captain came out on the bridge and said, 'Lads!
'We're all doomed . . .
'The 'ole tub's goin' down.
'To the boats. Every man. Except you.' I said,
    'Me?' He said,
'Yes, there's no room, you must drown.'
I said 'Drown?' He said, '*Drown*; the 'ole ship's
    goin' down,
'Don't stand arguin' there,
'I've just told you straight
'There's not room for you mate,
'On the boats or in fact anywhere.
'I know it's upsetting
'But what's the use fretting?
'We might have lost all of the crew;
'But *now*, as I say,
'We can all get away,
'And only lose one, and that's you.'

Biographical Notes

Adele Aldridge (1934–   )

An American illustrator and pioneer of 'visual poetics', Adele Aldridge is the creator of 'Notpoems'.

Woody Allen (1935–   )

One of the funniest contemporary American screen comedians, Woody Allen belongs to the *genre* of funny-men forever insecure and finding the outside forces too great to cope with. Was once a gag-writer; writes, directs and acts in his own films.

Richard Harris Barham (1788–1845)

Born in Canterbury and educated at Brasenose College, Oxford, Barham became a minor churchman of St Paul's. Remembered as the author of the *Ingoldsby Legends*. He wrote comic and often grotesque verses which enjoyed great popularity in their day.

Beachcomber (J. B. Morton) (1893–1979)

Although *The Times* in its obituary managed to confuse J. B. Morton the humorist with H. V. Morton the travel writer, this only shows that the spirit of Beachcomber lingers on. His unique column appeared for many years in the London *Daily Express*. 'Pure Beachcomber' often describes situations of manifest absurdity.

Max Beerbohm (1872–1956)

English writer and caricaturist (known in London circles as 'the incomparable Max'), Beerbohm's most famous book is *Zuleika Dobson* — a story of Oxford life. He was married to an American actress, Florence Kahn. Writer of many brilliant essays.

Hilaire Belloc (1870–1953)

Joseph Hilaire Peter Belloc, born in France of a French father and English mother. Served in French forces, and later came to finish his education at Oxford. Once sat as Liberal MP — but perhaps best remembered for his humorous verses, especially *Cautionary Tales*.

Robert Benchley (1889–1945)

Born in Worcester, Massachusetts and educated at Harvard. Dramatic critic of *New Yorker* and a prolific contributor to the magazine. Acted in and wrote motion picture comedies. His books include *20,000 Leagues under the Sea, or, David Copperfield*.

John Betjeman (1906–)

Educated at Marlborough and Oxford where he was contemporary with Auden and MacNeice. Authority on industrial and railway architecture. Received the Queen's Medal for Poetry, the CBE and was made Poet Laureate in 1973. Not primarily a nonsense writer.

Niels Mogens Bodecker (1922–)

Born in Copenhagen, 'Bo' Bodecker creates a special world of the absurd in his word and picture books. He has worked as a cartoonist and illustrator in Denmark and the U.S.A.

Gyles Brandreth (1948–)

A contemporary journalist and author with a fondness for breaking records. As well as writing the shortest poem in world history, he has tossed the world's tiniest pancake (1mm in diameter) and made the world's longest after-dinner speech, talking non-stop for eleven hours.

Gelett Burgess (1866–1951)

Born in Boston, Massachusetts, Frank Gelett Burgess wrote many humorous books and introduced the word 'blurb' into the language. ('Self-praise; to make a noise like a publisher'). Worked as a draughtsman for the Southern Pacific Railway and instructor in topographical drawing at the University of California.

Robert Burns (1759–96)

Scottish poet of genius and much loved (especially by women). He was put early to the plough, which together with his other weakness (tippling) undermined his health. Writer of many love-songs, and, of course, *Auld Lang Syne*.

Douglas Byng (1893–   )

Actor and comedian, born in Nottinghamshire; once designed theatrical costumes, and performed in Concert Parties between the Wars. He graduated to the famous Gaiety Theatre, and became a cabaret entertainer and revue star, his speciality being female impersonation.

George Canning (1770–1827)

Educated at Eton and Oxford, and entered Parliament in 1793. Became Prime Minister in 1827 but died a few months later. Primarily a serious poet, his *Collected Poems* were published in 1823.

Henry Carey (1687?–1743)

Poet and musician — believed to be an illegitimate son of George Savile, Marquis of Halifax. His best known poem is 'Sally in Our Alley'. He wrote innumerable witty poems, farces and burlesques.

Lewis Carroll (Charles Dodgson) (1832–98)

The Reverend Charles Lutwidge Dodgson spent his working life as an Oxford don, teaching mathematics at Christ Church. As Lewis Carroll, the creator of the immortal Alice, he is recognised as perhaps the greatest of all English nonsense writers.

G. K. Chesterton (1874–1936)

Gilbert Keith Chesterton, born in London of an English father and French-Scottish mother. Educated at St Paul's, and the Slade School of Art. Wrote many works of literary criticism and verse, as well as his Father Brown detective stories. Illustrated the works of his friend Hilaire Belloc.

Samuel Taylor Coleridge (1772–1834)

The youngest of thirteen children, went to school at Christ's Hospital with Charles Lamb. He became friendly with the poet Southey (they married sisters) and settled in Somerset, where Wordsworth was his neighbour. Here he wrote 'The Rime of the Ancient Mariner' and 'Kubla Khan' and (with Wordsworth) the Lyrical Ballads. He became addicted to opium.

Frank Davies (1911–   )

Not known to be related to Fred Davies the erstwhile snooker champion, but has many kinsmen in Wales, notably Davies the Milk in Abergele and Davies the School in Cardiff.

John Davies of Hereford (1565?–1618)

Poet and writing-master. Wrote many un-nonsense books with titles like *The Triumph of Death* (a description of the Plague). Was famous in his day for his epigrams.

Charles Dickens (1812–70)

Born near Portsmouth where his father was a clerk in the Navy, his early life was full of hardship and his schooling inadequate. David Copperfield's experiences in the blacking factory are based on Charles Dickens' own experience. His literary career, once started, was a success story, and his public readings in America were popular and financially rewarding. He is likened to Shakespeare for the variety of his characters.

W. C. Fields (1879–1946)

William Claude Dukinfield, was born in Philadelphia. He started in vaudeville, and was a star of the Ziegfeld Follies. It is probably by now no secret that he was an alcoholic and misanthrope — and died on Christmas Day to prove it. His sad, mottled face showed the dismal view he had of mankind, and perhaps the surprising thing is that he was one of the most lugubriously funny men the American cinema has produced.

Samuel Foote (1720–77)

Actor and dramatist, born in Cornwall. Educated at Worcester College, Oxford, and lived as an eighteenth-century playboy until his fortune gave out, when he turned actor. He became a success as a comedian. He lost a leg after falling from a horse.

W. S. Gilbert (1836–1911)

William Schwenck Gilbert was born in London (his middle name was bequeathed him by his godmother). He was entered at the Inner Temple but the legal life was not rewarding enough. His fame came with the comic operas he wrote with Sir Arthur Sullivan. As a child Gilbert was kidnapped by bandits in Italy and was ransomed for the sum of £25.

A. D. Godley (1856–1925)

Alfred Denis Godley, son of an Irish rector, was educated at Harrow and Balliol. Fellow of Magdalene and a classical scholar. Wrote several volumes of witty verse, notably *Verses to Order* as well as more serious works.

Oliver Goldsmith (1728–74)

Another son of an Irish clergyman. Was disfigured by smallpox as a child. Destined for the church as a profession, he rebelled against the parental choice and managed to be unacceptable. Went on a walking tour of Europe — and later secured a medical degree. Perhaps his best known novel is *The Vicar of Wakefield*. Though feckless, he was well loved by his friends.

Harry Graham (1874–1936)

Harry Jocelyn Clive Graham, educated at Eton and Sandhurst — prolific writer of humorous verse and prose, now remembered almost exclusively for his *Ruthless Rhymes for Heartless Homes*.

Robert Graves (1895–   )

Born in London, Robert Ranke Graves has been a soldier, shop-keeper, poet, critic and historical novelist. Educated at Charterhouse and St John's College, Oxford, he was Professor of Poetry at Oxford 1961–6. In 1926 he was Professor of English at Cairo University.

W. Heath Robinson (1896–1944)

Simply one of the most original, inventive and eccentric English illustrators of the century. Has brought into currency the expression 'Heath Robinsonish' to describe fantastic mechanical contrivances.

A. P. Herbert (1890–1971)

Born in London and educated at Winchester and Oxford. MP for Oxford University in 1936. His many campaigns included agitation for Authors' Lending Rights, and against jargon and officialese. Also contributor to *Punch*. Knighted in 1945.

Dr Heinrich Hoffman (1809–94)

A Victorian humorist, Hoffman is now chiefly remembered for his 'Cautionary Verses' in the tradition of Hilaire Belloc.

Gerard Hoffnung (1925–59)

Musical comedian and cartoonist, was responsible for the popular Hoffnung Music Festival Concerts held at the Royal Festival Hall in London. The highlights of these concerts were the playing of house-hold and garden artefacts (such as hoses and bottles) as musical instruments. Made irreverent fun of musical instruments and orchestras, and once played the largest tuba in England in public.

Oliver Wendell Holmes (1809–94)

Born in Cambridge, Massachusetts, he studied medicine at Harvard and in Paris. Became Professor of Anatomy at Dartmouth and at Harvard Medical School. Famous for his 'Breakfast Table' talks. He received honorary degrees from Oxford, Cambridge and Edinburgh.

A. E. Housman (1859–1936)

Educated at Bromsgrove School and St John's College, Oxford.
Served as a clerk in the Patent Office, but later was appointed to the
Chair of Latin at University College, London, then to the same post in
Cambridge. His best known poem is 'A Shropshire Lad'.

Ted Hughes (1930–   )

Born in Yorkshire — and one of the few contemporary English poets
known to the 'man in the street'. Has been a powerful influence on
English poetry for the last twenty years.

Christoper Isherwood (1904–   )

Christopher William Bradshaw Isherwood, born at Disley, in
Cheshire. Studied medicine at King's, London. Was a contemporary of
Auden with whom he travelled to China and the United States. In
1946 he became an American citizen.

ITMA by Ted Kavanagh (1894–1958)

It's That Man Again was *the* British wartime radio comedy. It starred
Tommy Handley and its many catch-phrases became part of the
currency of wartime humour. Still held in deep affection by every
Briton over the age of forty-five.

Paul Jennings (1918–   )

Journalist and author, Paul Jennings was the first humorist to write a
column, *Oddly Enough*, in the *Sunday Observer*. He also writes books
for children (and has six of his own).

Samuel Johnson (1709–84)

Lexicographer, critic and poet, Samuel Johnson was the son of a
Lichfield (Staffordshire) bookseller. He went to Pembroke College in
1728 but owing to poverty had to leave without taking a degree.
Apart from his famous *Dictionary of the English Language*, which took
him ten years to compile, he is remembered as a great social personality and witty observer of life, for which we are ever in debt to his
biographer, Boswell.

John Keats (1795–1821)

Born in London and qualified as a surgeon at Guy's Hospital. One of the great romantic poets and friend of Shelley and Leigh Hunt. He died at the age of twenty-five of consumption.

Stephen Leacock (1869–1944)

Stephen Butler Leacock was born in Hampshire, England, and when he was seven years old emigrated with his parents to Canada. He was educated at the University of Toronto, took his PhD in Chicago, then worked at McGill University. Though trained as a scientist and economist, he is surely best known for his Nonsense Novels.

Edward Lear (1812–88)

Born in London of Danish descent, he was one of fifteen children. Suffered from epilepsy and asthma, but became widely known as an artist and poet, and exhibited at the Royal Academy. He gave drawing lessons to Queen Victoria — we don't know whether the Queen was amused by his nonsense verses. We are indebted to him for the limerick.

John Lennon (1940–   )

One of the famous Liverpool 'Beatles' — writer, with Paul McCartney, of many of their famous songs. Writes prose and poetry and has instinctive sense of 'nonsense'.

Dan Leno (George Galvin) (1860–1904)

Born George Galvin, he began his career at the age of four, singing and dancing in public houses. Became famous for his pantomime Dames — particularly at Drury Lane. He died, insane, from overwork and loneliness soon after the death of his stage 'feed'.

C. S. Lewis (1898–1963)

Clive Staples Lewis, was born in Belfast, and educated at Malvern and University College, Oxford. Fellow of Magdalene and appointed Professor of Medieval and Renaissance English at Cambridge. Wrote several delightful children's books, including *The Lion, the Witch and the Wardrobe*.

Vachel Lindsay (1879–1931)

Nicholas Vachel Lindsay was born in Springfield, Illinois. He tramped through the West, making a living by reciting his ragtime poems, for hospitality.

Hugh Lofting (1886–1947)

Born in Maidenhead, Berkshire, and educated at a Jesuit college, he later studied at the Massachusetts Institute of Technology. Also worked as a civil engineer in Canada, Africa and the West Indies. Is perhaps best known for his stories of *Dr Doolittle* — played in the movie by Rex Harrison.

Archibald MacLeish (1892–   )

American poet born at Glencoe, Illinois, and educated at Yale and Harvard. Was Librarian of Congress 1939–44, and appointed Professor of Rhetoric at Harvard, 1949. Won the Pulitzer Prize for Drama in 1958, and at one time was scriptwriter for Franklin D. Roosevelt.

Walter de la Mare (1873–1956)

Walter John de la Mare, CH, OM, was born at Charlton, in Kent, and educated at St Paul's Cathedral Choir School. On his mother's side he was related to Robert Browning. For eighteen years he was a clerk in the offices of an oil company but in 1908 was granted a Civil List pension, enabling him to devote all his time to writing.

Don Marquis (1878–1937)

Donald Robert Perry Marquis, journalist and poet. He was born in Walnut, Illinois. Became a columnist for the New York *Sun* and is best remembered for his poems about archy, the cockroach, and mehitabel the cat. His more serious works were not so successful.

Roger McGough (1937–   )

Liverpool born, poet and member of the pop group Scaffold, gives readings of his own poetry and loves 'things funny'.

Spike Milligan (1918–)

Clown and eccentric extraordinaire, Terence Milligan was born in India. He is probably without equal in his vein of irreverent verbal surrealism, and was the guiding star behind *The Goon Show* on BBC. ('He walked with a pronounced limp, L-I-M-P, pronounced limp.')

Adrian Mitchell (1932–)

More than any other poet, he is probably responsible for the present popularity of poetry readings in England. He says he finds it more satisfactory to read to his audience than to see his work in print, and that the aim of his work is to 'change the world'.

Monty Python

You won't find any logical reasons for the name — the perpetrators of which are John Cleese, Graham Chapman, Terry Gilliam, Erid Idle, Terry Jones and Michael Palin. All are well known in their own right, and all clever in their eccentric and versatile fashion.

Edwin Morgan (1920–)

Born in Glasgow, and educated at Glasgow High School and Glasgow University. Served in the Second World War with the Royal Army Medical Corps. Now lectures in English at Glasgow University. His work has been widely anthologised.

Ogden Nash (1902–71)

Prolific poet of nonsense and light verse, Frederick Ogden Nash was born at Rye, New York State. Highly individualistic style with puns, clerihews, limericks — but there is often seriousness behind all the fun. Collaborated with S. J. Perelman and Kurt Weill in making the Broadway musical *One Touch of Venus*.

Flann O'Brien (1911–66)

The pseudonym of Brian O'Nolan. Born at Strabane, Ireland, and educated at Dublin, afterwards becoming a civil servant. His writing is a blend of humour, farce and fantasy. 'At Swim-Two-Birds' is considered to be his best work. Also used the pseudonym of Myles na Gopaleen.

Philip O'Connor (1916–)

Born in Leighton Buzzard, Bedfordshire, and educated partly in
France. He left school at sixteen and took up tramping around
Europe. Has edited his own magazine, *Seven*, and worked as script-
writer for the BBC.

Brian Patten (1946–)

Another Liverpool poet. Once edited the magazine *Underdog*. He says
he was put into a neat pigeon-hole, but flew out.

Mervyn Peake (1911–68)

Artist, poet and novelist, Mervyn Peake is well known for his novels
Titus Groan, *Titus Alone* and *Gormenghast*. He was an official war artist
in the Second World War.

John Phoenix (George H. Derby) (1824–61)

Is the pen name of George Horatio Derby, a Californian news-
paperman. In the very first rank of American humorists.

Sylvia Plath (1932–63)

Prolific American poet, was married to Ted Hughes.

Roger Price (1921–)

American illustrator and humorist.

Alexander Resnikoff (1894–)

Born in Brooklyn, and educated at the University of Missouri and
New York University Law School. In 1916 was admitted to the Bar
of the State of New York.

Moss Rich (1920–)

Moss Rich lives in England and is principal of the College of Ribaldry.

Robert Robinson (1927–)

Familiar to the British public as a witty and fluent chairman of various television and radio quizzes and contests.

Christina Rossetti (1830–94)

Sister to Dante Gabriel, and one of the Pre-Raphaelites. Much of her work is of a devotional and rather melancholy nature. ('Does the road wind uphill all the way? Yes to the very end . . .')

W. C. Sellar (?–1951) and R. J. Yeatman (?–1968)

Sellar and Yeatman met while at Oxford. They collaborated on several funny books, but *1066 And All That* stands out as a classic of 'howlers'.

Robert Service (1874–1958)

Robert William Service was born in Preston, but moved with his parents to Glasgow, and was educated at Hillhead High School and Glasgow University. He emigrated to Canada when a young man and became a reporter for the *Toronto Star*. He wrote 'The Shooting of Dangerous Dan McGrew'.

William Shakespeare (1564–1616)

William Shakespeare (known to some as Francis Bacon) was born (as if you didn't know) at Stratford-upon-Avon. Held by many to be the greatest genius of this or any other age. His life is not well documented, but it is known he had two brothers and four sisters.

Timothy Shy (D. B. Wyndham Lewis) (1894–1969)

Born in Wales and went to Oxford, which he left to serve as a private in the First World War. He was the first Beachcomber and Timothy Shy of the *News Chronicle* from 1934. He also made translations and studies of historical figures as well as an anthology called 'The Non-sensibus'.

Peter Simple (Michael Wharton) (1913–   )

Michael Wharton is the writer and editor of the *Daily Telegraph's* satirical 'Peter Simple' column. His characters, such as Julian Birdbath, the literary critic who lives at the bottom of a mine, are immortals in the Beachcomber tradition.

N. F. Simpson (1919–   )

Educated at Emmanuel School and Birkbeck College, University of London. His play *A Resounding Tinkle* won a prize in the *Observer* play competition, 1957. He also wrote a play where a man tries to teach a large choir of Speak-Your-Weight machines to sing Handel's Messiah.

John Skelton (1460–1529)

There is some doubt as to whether John Skelton was Poet Laureate to Henry VIII but he certainly held that position in the Universities of Oxford and Cambridge. In later life he attacked corruption in the church and insulted Cardinal Wolsey. He was forced to take sanctuary in Westminster, where he remained until his death.

Stevie Smith (1903–71)

Had a gift for robbing prosaic phrases of their banality. She wrote a poem about a sea-side tragedy with the oft-quoted line 'Not waving but drowning'. She also wrote three novels in addition to a great output of poetry.

Jonathan Swift (1667–1745)

Born in Dublin of English parents, and brought up in circumstances of extreme poverty. He went to Trinity College, Dublin, but did not become a keen student until he acted as secretary to Sir William Temple, at his home in Farnham, Surrey. He is buried in St Patrick's Cathedral. Probably best remembered for *Gulliver's Travels*.

William Makepeace Thackeray (1811–63)

One of the greatest of English novelists. Born in Calcutta, he was educated at Charterhouse and Trinity College, Cambridge, but left without taking a degree. Had a life of many vicissitudes. Was a friend of Tennyson. Perhaps his best known work is *Vanity Fair*.

Dylan Thomas (1914–53)

Born in Swansea, Wales, Dylan Marlais Thomas was a grammar-school boy and worked for a time as a reporter on the South Wales *Evening Post*. He attracted a large following, particularly among young people, and became a 'cult' figure. He died during a lecture tour of the United States.

J. R. R. Tolkein (1892–1973)

John Ronald Reuel Tolkein was Merton Professor of English Language and Literature. He published philosophical and critical works, as well as the well known *Hobbit* and the *Ring* books.

Mark Twain (Samuel Clemens) (1835–1910)

This was the pen name of Samuel Langhorne Clemens, and had been used earlier in the *New Orleans Picayune* by Isaiah Sellers. It was an expression used on the Mississippi steamers to indicate two fathoms. As well as *Tom Sawyer*, and *Huckleberry Finn* he was also a travel writer. ('Foreigners always spell better than they pronounce'.)

Stanley Unwin (1911–   )

A famous English television 'professor' who has evolved a kind of verbal scribble which we somehow manage to understand. He makes as much (if not more) sense than some of the learned experts who speak the Queen's English.

John Updike (1932–   )

American novelist and poet, born in Shillington, Pennsylvania. Educated there, at Harvard, and at the Ruskin School of Drawing, Oxford. Has also written short stories and essays and was a reporter on the magazine, the *New Yorker*.

J. J. Webster (1920–)

English humorous poet, lives in Enfield, Middlesex, and deserves to be more widely known.

Edward Reed Whittemore (1919–)

Born in New Haven, Connecticut and educated at Yale and Princeton. During the Second World War served in USAAF. Since 1969 has been literary editor of the Washington *New Republic*. Consultant in poetry to the Library of Congress. He explains that he sides with those who stand on the sidelines of the game in progress and make frosty remarks instead of cheering.

T. H. White (1906–64)

Terence Hanbury White, English writer whose popular reputation rests on his Arthurian trilogy, *The Once and Future King*. Also wrote an account of how he trained a hawk, called *The Goshawk*.

Robb Wilton (1881–1957)

Robb Wilton was one of the stalwarts of wartime radio in Britain with his witty and ridiculous sketches. One of his most famous was the highly disorganised Fire Chief ('We'll have to get a telephone in here — there must be a lot of fires we never hear about . . .').

Index of Titles and First Lines

A Dirge, 23
A Fancy, 21
A Folk Song, 55
A Grotesque, 118
A Hum, 126
A little child was sitting, 192
All Our Yesterdays, 100
A muvver was barfin' 'er biby one night, 26
And the woman who lived next door, 211
And this reft house is that the which he built, 99
A Note on the Einstein Theory, 63
Another ludicrous scene occurred while Mr Tinklebury
    Snapdriver, 59
Apes and men had a common ancestor, 100
Apples, 208
A Python I should not advise, 67
Around, around the sun we go, 157
A sail on the sea, 221
As It Fell upon a Day, 21
As I was sitting on the hearth, 21
As oi wur a-waalkin' boi Bolzover Green, 58
A Song of Myself, 135
Asparagus, 208
At breakfast I had an innermost thought, 168
At Least It's a Precaution against Fire, 202
A Tragic Story, 210
Augustus was a chubby lad, 122
Awake, My Lute! 153
A. Was an Archer, 22
A. was an Archer, and shot at a frog, 22
Ay, beshrew you! by my fay, 204

Back Answers, 221
Be not sparing, 210
Born 1863. Only child of Ethel Cox, Virgin birth, 164

Caesar Invades Britain, 189
Captain Busby, 175
Captain Busby put his beard in his mouth and sucked it, 175
Charming Oysters I cry, 209
Come, buy my fine Oranges, Sauce for your Veal, 210
Come, buy my fine Wares, 208
Come, follow me by the Smell, 209
Come, let's to bed, says Sleepy-head, 24
Contract, Expand, and Explode, 190
Coughing in a shady grove, 82

Darius the Mede was a king and a wonder, 154
Death of My Aunt, 26
Doggerel, 188
Dorset, 73
Down in a deep dark ditch sat an old cow, 28
Dr Newton with the crooked pince-nez, 118
Droodles (ill.), 186

Elegy on the Death of a Mad Dog, 115
Eternal nothingness is O.K. if you're dressed for it, 45

Father heard his Children scream, 117
Fishy Tale, 189

Galoshes, 134
Gammer Gurton's Garland, 24
Gay go up and gay go down, 24
Go Down, Sweet Jordan, 70
Good King Arthur, 24
Good morning. Mrs Paradock? 202
Good people all, of every sort, 115
Green, 158

Gub Gub's Book (1932), 156

Hallelujah! was the only observation, 127
Happy to be hairy, 167
He came to her in the afternoon, 198
Hello folks. 'Its That Man Again' and what a man, 129
Hermit Hoar, 135
Hermit hoar, in solemn cell, 135
Herrings, 210
Hexameter and Pentameter, 28
High Tide (ill.), 120
Holiday Memory, 211
House Flies, 74
Humpty Dumpty, 89

I am having a *rapprochement* with galoshes, 134
I drive my car to supermarket, 218
I Dunno, 31
If all the filth the seas provide, 80
If there were, oh! an Hellespont of cream, 100
If You Should Meet a Crocodile, 37
If you should meet a crocodile, 37
I have chambers up in Gray's-inn, 111
I Have My Price, 181
I have my price — it's rather high, 181
I knew a funny little man, 175
I'm a riddle in nine syllables, 185
I'm a stamp, 31
I met a Bishop in the street, 188
I never saw a Purple Cow, 75
In Memoriam Examinatoris Cuiusdam, 114
Instructions for Using Your Japanese Pocket Calculator, 187
In this connection I wish to say one word about Michael Angelo, 214
Ipecacuanha, 82

I Sat Belonely down a Tree, 151
I sat belonely down a tree, 151
I sometimes think I'd rather crow, 31
I stood in the gloom of a spacious room, 153
It is said that there are, 63
ITMA, 129
It was very strange that I should first meet my wife in the Maze, 151
I was born about ten thousand years ago, 30
I was sitting in my office, 39
I Waxes, and I Wanes, Sir, 181
I waxes, and I wanes, sir, 181
I Wish I Were, 33
I wish I were a, 33
I wrote some lines once on a time, 126

Jabberwocky, 87
Janet Was Quite Ill One Day, 30
Janet was quite ill one day, 30
John, an Awful King, 190
jollymerry, 169

Labour-Saving, 58
La Forza del Destino, 219
L'Enfant Glacé, 118
Let's think of eggs, 170
Letters, 85
Life Story, 35
Little Betty Winkle she had a pig, 23
Little Johnny's Confession, 178
Looking Glass Insects, 91
Love's Labour's Lost, 193
Lo, where you undistinguished grave, 114

Mannerly Margery Milk and Ale, 204
Merry Margaret, 205
Metaphors, 185
Millie the Mermaid, 80
Miss Rafferty wore taffeta, 172
Monty Python, 167
Mother Goose's Garland, 157
Mother Goose's Melody, 22
Mother's Lament, 26
Mr Big, 39
Mr Weller having obtained leave of absence, 101
My aged friend, Mrs Wilkinson, 158
My aunt she died a month ago, 26
My Philosophy, 45
My Uncle Dan, 128
My Uncle Dan's an inventor, you may think that's very fine, 128

Namby Pamby, 82
Naught Paughty Jack-a-Dandy, 82
Never Give a Sucker an Even Break, 107
Nicholas Nickleby, 106
Nonsense Botany, 147
Norman Henderson's Diary, 168
Now momma an' poppa they gotta ragazzo, 219
Now popes and persons, majesties and powers, 120

O, 75
Ode to My Goldfish, 75
O Here It Is and There It Is, 180
O here it is! and there it is! 180
Oh there hasn't been much change, 207
O Kangaroo, O Kangaroo, 173
Old Noah he had an ostrich farm and fowls on the largest scale, 98
O Love! O Death! O Ecstasy! 179
O Love! O Death! O Ecstasy! 179

On a small six-acre farm dwelt John Grist the miller, 27
Once a little boy, Jack, was, Oh! ever so good, 29
Once — but no matter when, 35
Once upon a time, a long while ago, 142
One fine October morning, 37
On mules we find two legs behind, 34
On the Death of a Female Officer of the Salvation Army, 127
On the fourth floor of the old house in the suburbs of Jazzcsyl, 197
On the Motor Bus, 114
*On the Subject of TV and Radio Reception and Hearing the News
    in Dutch*, 218
Onyons, 209
Oranges, 210
Our Italian Guide, 214
'Our second experiment,' the Professor announced, 97
Our service explained. Here is how it happened, 173
Our Stoves, 152
Oysters, 209

Phoenix's Pictorial, 182
Pickwick Papers, 101
Plum's Dying Speech, 120
Poor Beasts! 29
'*Pop Notes' by Jim Droolberg*, 200
Portrait of His Royal Highness Prince Albert, 182,

Quingwam quingwam, 99

Rat Recipes, 167
Realism, 201
Rhubarb Ted, 175
Rime Intrinsica, Fontmell Magna, Sturminster Newton
    and Melbury Bubb, 73
'Ripe 'Sparagrass, 208
Rufus. A Ruddy King, 191

Said the Duck to the Kangaroo, 140
Satellite is this fine, up shoot–F-t! 218
Sir Rupert the Fearless, A Legend of Germany, 46
Sir Rupert the Fearless, a gallant young knight, 46
Some people — not you nor I, 137
Something, probably diet, seems to have stunted my mental
     growth, 171
Somewhat Alike, 34
Song in Outer Esquimo Dialect, 99
So she went into the garden to cut a cabbage leaf, 111
Sporting Relations, 163
Stalemate, 55
Superman, 218
Sylvie and Bruno (1889), 97
Sylvie and Bruno (1893), 97

Take honble Thing and press her twice, 187
Take four medium-sized rats, 167
Tale of a Stamp, 31
Tam O'Shanter, 75
1066 And All That, 189
Ten Thousand Years Ago, 30
Tenuous and Precarious, 206
Tenuous and Precarious, 206
Test Paper III, 190
The Apeman's Hairy Body Song, 167
The Awful Fate of Melpomenus Jones, 137
The Bad Child's Book of Beasts and *More Beasts for Worse Children*, 66
The Bards, 158
The Bells of London, 24
The Best of Myles na Gopaleen, 173
The Bread-Knife Ballad, 192
The Case of the Twelve Red-Bearded Dwarfs, 59
The circumstances of archy's first appearance, 158
the coming of archy, 158

The Common Cormorant, 128
The common cormorant (or shag), 128
The Computer's First Christmas Card, 169
The Daniel Jazz, 154
The Dublin Waama League's Escort Service, 173
The Duck and the Kangaroo, 140
The Filthy Swine, 200
The first date in English History is 55 BC, 189
The Force of Destiny, 219
The Goon Show, 164
The Grand Panjamdrum, 111
The Grange, 207
The gum-chewing student, 34
The Hampton Court Maze, 151
The Horn (ill.), 125
The horse and the mule live thirty years, 29
The House That Jack Built, 99
The Irish Pig, 26
The Jumblies, 144
The Kangaroo, 173
The Last Laugh, 126
The Man in the Moon Stayed up Too Late, 212
The Man in the Wilderness, 21
The man in the wilderness asked of me, 21
The Marmozet, 66
The Myles na Gopaleen Catechism of Cliché, 174
The New Diving Boat (ill.), 119
The Organ (ill.), 124
The Owl and the Pussy-cat, 139
The owl and the pussy-cat went to sea, 139
The Party, 219
The Pig, 173
The pig, if I am not mistaken, 173
The Poultries, 170
The Private Dining-Room, 172
The Python, 67

The question is often asked in the Athenaeum Club, 196
The recent International Exhibition of Inventions, 58
There is an inn, a merry old inn, 212
There lived a sage in days of yore, 210
There was a book lying near Alice, 87
There was a naughty boy, 135
There was an old grocer of Goring, 158
There was a witch, 187
There used to be a time, 70
The Sad Story of the Little Boy That Cried, 29
The Secret Hill, 198
The Skate, 167
The species Man and Marmozet, 66
The Stern Parent, 117
The Stork's Nest, 197
The Story of Augustus, 121
The Story of the Four Little Children Who Went Round the World, 142
The Student, 111
The sun was shining on the sea, 92
The Tenor (ill.), 125
The Walrus and the Carpenter, 92
The Whango Tree, 36
The Winter's Tale, 196
The Witch's Work Song, 220
The woggly bird sat on the whango tree, 36
They served tea in the sandpile, together with, 219
They went to sea in a Sieve, they did, 144
'This is the first class in English spelling and philosophy,
   Nickleby', 106
This monarch was always very angry, 191
This morning, 178
Thoughts Thought While Resting Comfortably in Phillips House, 171
Three Notpoems (ill.), 38
Three wise men of Gotham, 22
'Tickets, please!' said the Guard, 91
'Tis sad to relate, 175

To Mary MacDonald — 5 Nov. 1864, 85
To Mistress Margaret Hussey, 205
'Twas an evening in November, 26
Two Legs Behind and Two Before, 34
Two spoons of sherry, 220
Two Witches, 187

Uncle Terry was a skydiver, 163
Under the Drooping Willow Tree, 27

Variations on a Simple Theme, 196
Verses Made for Women Who Cry Apples, &c, 208

Warble, child; make passionate my sense of hearing, 193
Well, to go back to Patricia Portly, 156
We're All in the Dumps, 24
We're all in the dumps, 24
What happens to blows at a council meeting? 174
What inclement weather, 107
What is this that roareth thus? 114
What makes, 74
What Nonsense! 37
When baby's cries grew hard to bear, 118
When chapman billies leave the street, 75
When daffodils begin to peer, 196
When fishes set umbrellas up, 189
When good King Arthur ruled this land, 24
When John came to the throne, 190
When Piecrust first began to reign, 21
When Piledriver Films took over the pretty village of Dorminster
    Monachorum, 201
When the curtain rises, the stage is in darkness. . ., 55
Where there is an article, 152
Williamanmary? England Ruled by an Orange, 192
Williamanmary for some reason was known as The Orange, 192
Wine and Water, 98

You must explain to me, please, the Professor said, 97
You seem very clever at explaining words, 89

Acknowledgments

The following are thanked for their permission to include copyright material:

William Heinemann Ltd for Arthur Rackham's illustration 'Three Wise Men of Gotham' from *Mother Goose Nursery Rhymes*.

Adele Aldridge for the three 'Notpoems' published by the Magic Circle Press. © Adele Aldridge 1973.

W. H. Allen & Co. Ltd and Random House Inc. for 'Mr Big' from *Getting Even* by Woody Allen. © Woody Allen 1973.

A. D. Peters & Co. Ltd for the four 'Beachcomber' pieces by J. B. Morton.

Sir Rupert Hart-Davis for 'A Note on the Einstein Theory' from *Mainly on Air* by Max Beerbohm. © Mrs Eva Reichmann.

Gerald Duckworth & Co. Ltd for 'The Marmozet' and 'The Python' from *The Bad Child's Book of Beasts* and *More Beasts for Worse Children* by Hilaire Belloc.

John Murray (Publishers) Ltd and Houghton Mifflin Co. for 'Dorset' from *Collect Poems* by John Betjeman.

J. M. Dent & Sons Ltd and Atheneum Publishers Inc. for 'House Flies' from *Hurry, Hurry Mary Dear* by N. M. Bodecker.

Dover Publications Inc. for the poem by Gelett Burgess from *The Burgess Nonsense Book*.

The Bodley Head and the author for 'Millie the Mermaid' from *Byng Ballads* by Douglas Byng.

The Estate of G. K. Chesterton for his poem 'Wine and Water'.

Frank Davies for his two poems.

Universal City Studios and Lorrimer Publishing Ltd for the extract from *Never Give a Sucker an Even Break*. © Universal City Studios 1941.

Edward Arnold (Publishers) Ltd for the illustrated poems from *Ruthless Rhymes for Heartless Homes* by Harry Graham.

Robert Graves for 'A Grotesque' from his *Collected Poems*.

Gerald Duckworth & Co. Ltd for the illustrations from *Devices* by W. Heath Robinson.

The Estate of A. P. Herbert for 'Plum's Dying Speech' from *Two Gentlemen of Soho* by A. P. Herbert.

Quentin Blake and Fontana Paperbacks Ltd for the illustrations to 'The Story of Augustus' by Dr Heinrich Hoffman.

The Estate of A. E. Housman, the Society of Authors, Jonathan Cape Ltd, and Holt, Rinehart and Winston for the poem by A. E. Housman.

Faber & Faber Ltd and the author for 'My Uncle Dan' from *Meet My Folks* by Ted Hughes.

Christopher Isherwood for his poem 'The Common Cormorant'.

P. J. Kavanagh for the extract from 'ITMA' by Ted Kavanagh.

The Bodley Head for 'Galoshes' from *Model Oddlies* by Paul Jennings.

The Bodley Head, Dodd, Mead & Co. and McLelland and Stewart Ltd for 'The Awful Fate of Melpomenus Jones' by Stephen Leacock from *The Bodley Head Leacock* and *Literary Lapses*.

Jonathan Cape Ltd and the author for 'I Sat Belonely' from *John Lennon in His Own Write*.

The Estate of C. S. Lewis for his poem 'Awake, My Lute!'

Macmillan Publishing Co. for 'The Daniel Jazz' by Vachel Lindsay. © Macmillan Publishing Co. 1920, renewed Elizabeth Lindsay 1948.

Curtis Brown Ltd for 'Mother Goose's Garland' by Archibald MacLeish.

Ernest Benn Ltd, Dodd, Mead & Co. and McGraw-Hill Ryerson Ltd for 'The Bread-Knife Ballad' by Robert Service.

The *Daily Telegraph* for the extracts from the Peter Simple column.

Curtis Brown Ltd and the author for the extract from *At Least It's a Precaution against Fire* by N. F. Simpson.

James MacGibbon, executor to Stevie Smith, for 'Tenuous and Precarious' from *The Collected Poems of Stevie Smith*, published by Allen Lane.

Punch for 'The Grange' by Stevie Smith.

The Trustees for the copyrights of the late Dylan Thomas for the extract from *Holiday Memory*.

George Allen & Unwin (Publishers) Ltd and Houghton Mifflin Inc. for the poem from *The Adventures of Tom Bombadil* by J. R. R. Tolkein.

Victor Gollancz Ltd and Harper and Row, Publishers, Inc. for 'Superman' from *The Carpentered Hen and Other Tame Creatures* by John Updike. © John Updike 1955.

J. J. Webster for his poem 'La Forza del Destino'.

The University of Minnesota Press and the author for 'The Party' by Reed Whittemore.

David Higham Associates for 'The Witch's Work Song' from *The Sword in the Stone* by T. H. White, published by William Collins Sons & Co. Ltd.